THE ACCIDENTAL PLUS ONE

Travel Tales from a Trailing Spouse

ALISON RIPLEY CUBITT

Lambert Nagle Media

Copyright © 2024 by Alison Ripley Cubitt
All rights reserved.
No part of this book may be reproduced in any form or by any electronic or mechanical means, including information storage and retrieval systems, without written permission from the author, except for the use of brief quotations in a book review.

DEDICATION
For Susan Ripley and Philip Taylor, Kat Parker, James Underwood—our support crew who held the fort, while we led this crazy boomerang life.

DISCLAIMER
This book is based on my personal memories and experiences. While I've tried to recount events accurately, please keep in mind that memory can be fallible and that some dialogue has been recreated. To protect the privacy of individuals, names, places, or dates may have been changed.

1

The Job Interview

February 2000

My imaginary conversation with Nobel laureate TS Eliot as I crawl along Oxford Road, Manchester goes like this:

No, Thomas Stearns, the cruellest month isn't April. It's February here in the North West, when I can't see past the car in front.

Freezing fog passes for daylight at this time of the year. I've left and returned home in the dark all winter on my three-hour daily commute. And today is no different. If I'm not careful, I'll be doing this for the rest of my working life.

The fog clears by mid-morning and turns to rain that smashes against my office window. I glance down at the stick figures below, scurrying along with umbrellas aloft, like a scene out of an LS Lowry painting. When I next look up at the clock, it's 12.30pm. I grab my coat and umbrella and make for the door. It's still raining, but lunchtimes are my only chance to get any exercise during the working week.

As it's Monday—when senior jobs in advertising, broadcasting and media education are advertised—I buy a copy of the *Guardian*. I'm not looking to move jobs, but I want to know what's out there. As the rain pelts down, I hurry back to work, shaking off the water as I run up to the canteen to buy lunch, then to my office to eat *al desko* while looking at the job ads.

I turn straight to the media section. A display ad, with the words Media Professor New Zealand, jumps out at me. I think of my other half, known as BB Lookalike or Not Bryan Brown after a drunk in a sleazy bar in Montreal mistook him for the Australian actor. An assistant professor for ten years, he maybe needs to leave or threaten to do so to get promoted to full professor.

There aren't many universities in New Zealand. I've studied at three of them—graduating from Victoria in Wellington, a place I left 20 years ago, with an arts degree. And BB Lookalike's only connection to the country is through me. We spent a Christmas and New Year there, and one highlight was walking in the Abel Tasman National Park, not far from Mariri, where I grew up. It's a bit of a leap from going on holiday and liking a place, to applying for a job there, so I set aside this fantasy and examine the practicalities.

The job is in Hamilton at the University of Waikato. Despite being on the main highway between Wellington and Auckland, it's a place I've never wanted to stop at. And the friends who grew up there have all left. Known as a "cow town," it's smack in the middle of the North Island and prime dairy farming country.

How bad can it be? At least it's driving distance to the bright lights of Auckland.

At 5.45pm, my boss walks into my office. 'On your way,' he says. 'We don't get paid for overtime.'

When I've been here as long, I'll turn into a clock watcher like you.

'I'm waiting for the traffic to clear,' I fib. In reality, I'm agonising over a Catch-22. In one corner is an agent who wants a fee we can't afford. In the other, a producer who is pressuring me to pay what they're asking, and in the third, the boss who says we've reached the payment ceiling. And I'm the one who has to get them to all agree.

Things must be bad if sitting in a traffic jam is preferable to answering another passive-aggressive email from the entertainment department. I log out of my computer, sling the newspaper into my bag, grab my coat, and head out the door.

Once I'm clear of the city centre and on the M56, after the Manchester Airport turnoff, the traffic flows and I make good progress. I roll up at the home of Sue, our dogsitter, and as usual, Zebedee is reluctant to leave after hanging out with other dogs all day.

When we finally get home, the first thing I do is show BB Lookalike the ad.

'What do you reckon?'

'I'll have a look,' he says. 'I'll see if anyone knows anything about the department.'

When I have a spare moment, I weigh up the cost of living and the price of houses in England versus New Zealand. But I'm not comparing apples with apples, as the North West is one of the cheapest places to live here. Or I am, as Hamilton is comparable. The only difference is New Zealand has no stamp duty on property purchases.

BB Lookalike says he'll throw his hat in the ring and see what happens. Applying for jobs at other universities is expected when you've been at the same institution for a long time.

Two weeks after the closing date, Waikato invites BB

Lookalike to an in-person interview. In New Zealand. I want to go with him on a "look-see" visit, but I have neither the money nor the flexibility at work to take a holiday at such short notice. Because he leaves on a Saturday, I can drop him off at Manchester Airport. But as I can only park in the five-minute drop-off bay, we have to say our goodbyes in front of the parking warden, who strides towards us, telling me to hurry.

'Take plenty of pics,' I call as I zoom out of the parking spot before the grumpy attendant can book me.

I spend my days coming up with sweeteners, persuading a reluctant agent to go with the BBC rather than ITV for the sake of their client's future career. I can't pay the client what they ask for, but I can throw in a clothing allowance and their preferred hair and make-up artist. By night, I imagine myself walking on a deserted beach on the other side of the world.

Midweek, BB Lookalike calls me from his hotel. 'You'll love it here,' he says. He's come back from a tour of the countryside with one of the staff in the film and media department. She's taken him to Raglan on the West Coast, known throughout the surfing world as having one of the best left-hand breaks.

'It's how I imagine California was before it was ruined,' he says. 'There is a guy here from Hawaii who runs a burger bar and will never return.'

I pick him up from Manchester Airport the following Sunday. If he was offered the job, he'd say yes because he can shape the department and run with it. It's his chance to make a difference in a country with a population the size of Ireland's.

He's been back for fewer than twelve hours when the verbal offer comes through.

It's madness to up sticks and move to the other side of the world because we're sick of the weather and the climate in the UK. We both suffer from a form of seasonal affective disorder (SAD), but then, doesn't everybody? And what about the upheaval? Surely it's easier to find new jobs in England.

One of the many things BB Lookalike and I have in common is we are boarding school survivors. No experience will be as traumatic as the first night in the dormitory, lying awake, listening to all the other children weeping under the bedclothes and pining for home. Having the rug pulled out from under you when you're seven forces you to stand on your own two feet. We're both seasoned independent travellers, living abroad after graduating from university. And we thrive on change. The difference is this time, we'll be going on an adventure together.

New Zealand is my past, but could it be our future, too?

I scribble a note to say yes; in principle, subject to the fine print in the contract.

When the written contract comes through, we realise the salary will be enough for us to live on. And there's a generous relocation package. The university will pay us to take all our furniture and effects, cover our airfares, and give us six weeks in short-term accommodation. Of course, we must cover the cost of dog transport and vet checks for Zebedee, which will be more than both our flights combined.

'What do you think?'

'Yes,' I say. 'We left London and made it work. We can

make it happen in New Zealand too. The timing's right. For both of us.'

With a stroke of a pen, BB Lookalike signs his contract. The start date is another seven and a half months away.

And so, the countdown begins.

2

Wanted Down Under

Seven and a half months would be enough time to arrange a long-haul move, if this was our only major event. But in ten weeks' time, we'll become Mr and Mrs. We've been together fourteen years and thought it was about time we got hitched, although one of our engagement cards quips, 'Are you sure you aren't rushing into this?' At last, I'll be able to call myself The Wife of Bryan.

As well as a commuter with a full-time job, I'm the wedding planner and executive chef. Although the ceremony will take place at the Grosvenor in Chester, the only reception we can afford is a DIY one at our flat. I'm not daft enough to take on all the cooking myself, and I rope in as many friends as possible. As neither of us plays by the rules of convention, BB Lookalike will have a best woman rather than a best man and my bridesmaids are a mixture of friends and family.

Meanwhile, not long after we say yes to the job offer in New Zealand, I am called into a meeting with my boss and HR.

If they were firing me, they'd have given me a verbal and a written warning, so what's this all about?

They're not firing me, far from it. My boss is retiring, and HR wants to offer me the position of Head of Artists' Contracts. They dangle more money and an executive parking space in the underground car park inside the BBC building, which is the carrot I'm more excited about. Every evening after work, I psych myself up to walk alone in the dark to the outdoor car park, across the street and behind Oxford Road station. It is unmanned, and several BBC staff have been mugged or had their cars broken into.

I'm poker-faced as I accept the job. The pay rise is still nowhere near what I was getting as a freelancer, but it's a relief to know we'll have extra money to pay for our big do.

On the morning of our wedding day, in the middle of having my hair done, I am on the phone issuing instructions about the catering. My bible is *Party Food* by star caterer Lorna Wing. Some recipes are too fiddly and take three times as long as they should. But what can I expect? Lorna has a team of professional chefs where I've roped in amateur cooks. One guest is busy peeling pistachios for the jewelled rice, but I forgot to tell him they're only a garnish.

'How many pounds of pistachios do you need?' he asks.

Pounds? I didn't mean deplete the entire Turkish nut crop.

'Don't worry, we'll hand the rest out for the nibbles,' I say.

Once the formal ceremony at the Chester Grosvenor is over, we head back to West Kirby for the reception. At least I've had the sense to hire catering staff to set up the tables, pour the drinks and dish out the food. We put the champagne in the bath, which is full of ice, but this doesn't work out quite as we'd planned.

During the reception, one of the catering team whispers to me, 'We have a problem. You need to come and look.'

I go upstairs to find teenagers, most if not all related to me, swigging the champagne out of bottles. They have been setting a poor example, as I notice some tipsy children and go to alert the parents. While the parents sort out their offspring, we retrieve the remaining champagne to take down to the fridge in the kitchen before they can drink the joint dry.

That evening, my new husband and I head back to the Chester Grosvenor to stay the night, leaving the caterers to clean up. Pixies will tidy and do the washing up, while we relish the chance to escape. We spend a leisurely morning over breakfast before returning home, which is now immaculate. It can't have been easy. Our place is on the top three floors of a subdivided house, a type of flat known as a maisonette with private access. Someone would have had to lug rubbish bags and bottles down three flights.

The following day, we're both back at work.

I return to my Countdown to the Big Move, putting the dog's name at the top of my long to-do list. You can see I have my priorities right... But joking aside, exporting a pet to New Zealand is lengthy and bureaucratic. I need a seven-month window to complete the vaccinations, vet tests and export documents.

To comply with New Zealand and Australia's strict biosecurity laws, airlines don't allow pets in the aircraft cabin and put them in the animal hold. This is a separate part of the plane and is heated, unlike the baggage compartment, which isn't. We either have to re-home our dog or live with the guilt of knowing Zebedee will travel alone on an aircraft for 24 hours. Other pets may accompany her, each secured in their own containers, but except at the halfway stop in Singapore, where she will receive fresh water, she will not have any human contact. It's not a choice I want to make, but I console myself she is young, fit, bold, and adventurous.

I turn my attention to the New Zealand Residency Application. Despite growing up and living in New Zealand for 13 years, I travelled backwards and forwards on a British passport and never applied for citizenship. When I moved to Australia in my early twenties, I realised I had made a big mistake, but by then, it was too late to do something about it. And because I stayed out of the country for too long, the government revoked my residency. It has come back to haunt me, as now I must apply for residency, like any other hopeful immigrant, which runs on a points system and a quota. Fortunately, we meet the required points and our application is approved.

We are given three-year visas, which allow us to enter and leave the country as often as we wish. After five years, we can apply for permanent residency, followed by citizenship. I will never take the right to live and work in another country for granted again.

Now our immigration status is sorted, opening a bank account is the next thing we need to do. We contact ASB, which has a branch in London where we can deposit money and transfer it ready for our arrival, but we can't take any out until we get to New Zealand and present our passports to prove our identities.

With the pet relocation paperwork sorted, we speak to the specialist pet exporter we have hired, who advises us to train Zebedee to sleep in a cage like the one she will travel in. They drop one off three months before her departure date. We set it up in the living room and leave the cage door open, putting her treats and toys in there. It doesn't take long for her to get used to sleeping in it.

One of our important decisions is what to do with our maisonette—rent it out or sell it. If we choose to rent, we must do the same in Hamilton. If we sell, we will have the capital for a deposit and be eligible for a mortgage. A lousy experience of renting out our flat when we were both travelling for work has put us off. The nightmare tenants (who were friends of a friend) reneged on our mutual agreement of a six-month fixed-term contract and refused to move out when we told them we were returning.

We decide to sell.

If it all goes wrong and we return to the UK, we'll need to be closer to London, where most jobs are. So there seems to be little point in hanging on to our flat. I must also sell my investment property. This may not be a wise decision, but I'm still yet to find an estate agent to manage what is supposed to be my future pension. The flat is a minute's walk from my office, so when there are problems, I can go there during my lunch hour. I don't need the hassle of being a long-distance landlord.

Because it's a government department and I feel little loyalty to my place of work, I leave it to the last possible moment to hand in my notice. I've gone as far as I want to at the BBC. I spent years applying for jobs at the corporation and getting knocked back, so when I was successful, it took some time to sink in. But it didn't take long for the novelty to wear off and I have no desire to work in television again, at least not as a manager. And I'm not bothered about finding work straight away in New Zealand. There's enough to sort out finding and setting up our new home and a social life half a world away.

3

Them Southerners

West Kirby, November 2000
It's 7.30am, and there's a distinct late-autumn chill in the air. The leaves from the liquidambar tree form a slippery mulch on the driveway, and I weave my way carefully through them towards the taxi as it pulls up.

It's so me to go arse over tit in my travelling outfit.

I manage to stay upright. But as we load our luggage, the weather drizzles. We turn out of The Oatlands cul-de-sac and I take one last look at the flat. I'll miss the west-facing sitting room and the sun setting over Hilbre Island, but I'll take the memories we've made there with me. I remember our wedding day and the time Zebedee sneaked into the pantry and ate a dinner party's worth of goat cheese starters.

Once the movers had packed up and the flat was empty of our belongings, it was no longer home, and now it's up to the estate agent to manage the sale. The rain is sheeting down as we leave West Kirby and wind our way through Caldy, then past Arrowe Park. As we merge onto the M53, the spray and standing water slow the cautious drivers. But once we hit the M56, the volume of traffic and the speed freaks both increase exponentially.

I sit back in the taxi, a silly grin on my face. We're playing truant—skiving off when we both should be at work.

I glance at the passenger-side mirror to see a driver tailgating our taxi, flashing their fog lights. If our driver has to brake, the car behind will rear-end us. The tailgater pulls out to overtake, but misjudges the gap between us and the car in front and is inches from side-swiping our cab. And because there's nothing like a near-death experience to set your life flashing backwards, I timeshift 11 years.

Village on the border of Lancashire and Yorkshire, 1989

As I plonk the bottle of Gordon's gin on the counter, Tina looks me up and down.

'Having a party, are we?' she says, in a broad Lancashire accent.

As she rings up the till, I stall for time. If I answer yes, I'll underscore her suspicions I get up to no good when BB Lookalike is away in Liverpool, where he now works. A flat-out denial will lead her to believe I turn to drink as a coping mechanism because I can't stand my own company. While Tina has her suspicions about me, I return the favour.

What's a woman who gets up every morning to blow dry her immaculate bob, dyed the colour of Bournville chocolate, doing running the corner shop?

'You know, stocking up for the weekend,' I say, the gin bottle now wrapped in a brown paper bag and tucked under my arm. I watch my step on the uneven path as I walk four doors down the hill to our rented weaver's cottage.

We're in this village trying out country life, after getting together three years ago in London, a place we can no longer afford. I thought this relocation from down south to up north would be easy. I've worked in Lancashire, Tyneside, Yorkshire and Scotland—how much more "up north" can I get? And even though we're only half an hour away from happening Manchester, as soft Southerners, we're struggling to get used to the rural isolation.

Whether we like it or not, we are the blow-ins from London. When our friends visit and ask for directions in Tina's shop, she replies, 'You mean them Southerners at Number Four?' Even if we stay here 20 years, we'll be forever known by that nickname.

Manchester, 2000

As the plane takes off for Auckland via Singapore in the mist and the murk, I look out my window and guess we must be flying over the tiny rural village in the Pennines where everybody knows your name and your business.

Well, Tina, now we really are "Them Southerners."

After the thirteen-hour flight, we break our journey at Singapore for one night. "Asia Lite" is my favourite city for a stopover on my way Down Under, compared with traffic-clogged Bangkok and the concrete jungle of Kuala Lumpur. KL no longer feels familiar to me, even though I was born in Malaysia, because so many of the old buildings have been torn down and replaced with soulless modern high-rises. Singapore, once part of Malaysia, still feels a bit like coming home.

Instead of the honeymoon we never had, we have

splurged on a five-star hotel stay at Goodwood Park. Built by the same architect who designed Raffles, its park-like grounds are peaceful and relaxing after a long flight. We sip on Singapore Slings, luxuriate in the salt-water swimming pool, don waffle bath robes, and order room service.

I wonder how they're doing back in Artists' Contracts.

As the check-in for our onward flight to Auckland is at 10.25pm, we negotiate a late check-out. This gives us time for a leisurely hotel breakfast. Singapore's diverse food culture, where East meets West, is revealed as I pull up the silver cloches at the hotel breakfast buffet to see what's underneath. On one side is the Asian breakfast selection, ranging from Cantonese and Hainan-style noodle-based dishes, chicken with rice, and rice congee to Indian curries with roti bread. BB Lookalike chooses the Asian selection for his first course. I go for the Western breakfast and observe the chef working the egg section. I have yet to master the perfect omelette as BB Lookalike is so good at them. But I learn a few tips off the chef: hot pan, beat the eggs lightly, and pull the omelette together with a fork before flipping over and plating. From cracking the eggs to serving up takes fewer than two minutes.

Other guests, who can't decide which breakfast to choose, opt for both. One man has a portion of noodles with chicken and pairs it with a side order of bacon and eggs, followed by croissants and jam.

I make the most of the hotel facilities, from the gym to the pool, and order my favourite Hainanese chicken rice for lunch before our 3pm check-out. We leave our bags with the concierge, staying well away from the mayhem of Orchard Road shopping centre and head to the Singapore Museum instead, to kill time. We have the place to ourselves, and like our hotel, it's tranquil and what I need to prepare myself for another long-haul flight.

We return to the hotel at 5pm, order a cab and are at the airport by 5.45pm. It's still hours until our official check-in time, but Singapore Airlines allows us to check in early, and once we've offloaded our two suitcases apiece, we're free to take in all the sights at the airport, from the Butterfly House to designer shops. I use the time to get my 10,000 steps in, as the airport is the size of a small town. Then, tired out, we find the nearest bar and relax with a glass of champagne. It's still our mini-break, after all.

We buckle up at 12.25am, ready for the ten-hour flight to Auckland. Even after drinks and dinner, I'm still wide awake. On a long plane journey, I often take time to reflect, and tonight is no different.

London, 1980s

I'm working at my first job in television as a lowly production assistant when I hear about a party from a colleague. It's being held at the headquarters of the film and television union, an organisation to which you have to belong if you want a job in the industry. My flatmate and I swing by early, before the two other parties we plan to go to. There are no more than 50 people milling about in a venue with all the charm of a bus station, and the music is tasteful R&B.

Don't think much of the DJ. He's not even playing any dance music.

After a couple of drinks, I give up on the earnest discussions and am itching to boogie, but there's no dancing to R&B. Emboldened by the booze, I strut up to the DJ and ask, 'Got any Duran Duran or anything you can dance to?'

The DJ rolls his eyes as if to say, "Teenyboppers. What are they doing here?"

'No,' he says and turns away.

As the music is dreadful and the atmosphere worse, we bid farewell to the handful of people we know here and slip out into the nightlife of Covent Garden.

A few weeks later, I'm comatose in front of a late-night TV show on Channel 4. It's one of those "After the Pub Shuts" discussion programmes where earnest intellectuals talk about important stuff. Tonight, it's censorship in the media.* I want to switch to a music show, but I'm mesmerised. One pundit is wearing a salmon-pink jacket with only a vest on underneath.

Did they give the wardrobe department the night off? Hang on, where have I seen him before?

I'm sitting at my desk, headphones on, transcribing an interview, when in walks another visitor, the third we've had this morning. I pull off the headphones, then glance up. Dark hair, early-30s, kind of rakish.

'I'm here to view the rough cut,' he says in a London accent.

Not bad, way better than all the other hangers-on who tip up here.

'Yeah, sure, they're in here,' I say, ushering him into an office where a serious discussion about the rough cut is going on. There's drama in the office right now as we're over budget and there's a lot resting on the outcome of this edit.

As I walk back to my desk, I have an aha moment. (Not the band A-ha, but come to think of it, the visitor has hair a bit like Morten Harket's.) The DJ from the boring trade union party, the pink jacket off the telly, the visitor—they are one and the same person. When he comes out from the meeting, I'd better be nice to him, so he doesn't recognise me as the teenybopper who hated his music.

And here, dear reader, begins the reason why I'm on this plane with the love of my life, even though our music tastes are so different. What I didn't know then was his liking for Country, or what I call Dead Dog Music, a sub-genre of depressing songs on such topics as divorce, domestic abuse, homelessness, going to jail, and poverty. But can it get any worse? Yes it can, when the dog ups and leaves, or dies. I prefer electro-pop, anthems and upbeat music, including Duran Duran. Luckily, we can agree upon Crowded House, Echo and the Bunnymen, New Order, REM, The Mutton Birds, U2, and Van Morrison.

*(Comedians Mel Smith and Griff Rhys Jones parodied the discussion programme in their BBC comedy sketch show, *Alas Smith and Jones*.)

4

Help Me, Rhonda

After twelve hours in a flying tube with artificial light and recycled air, I stumble out into the dazzling sunshine, hand in front of my eyes. Even with sunglasses on, I'm squinting. I'd forgotten how harsh the Southern Hemisphere sun can be.

We spot our pre-booked minibus shuttle, which will take us to Hamilton. With two suitcases apiece, we take up all the luggage space. There isn't room to fit everything in the vehicle, so all the bags are piled into a trailer, which the driver hooks up to the bus. He pulls into the airport service station to get fuel, but a suitcase falls off as he turns. I swivel around to look. It's not one of ours.

Even though I'm jetlagged after the long flight, I take careful note of the layout of the airport, as I am due back here tomorrow to collect Zebedee. I also note the road and traffic volume as we drive State Highway 1 to Hamilton. It's been a long time since I've driven this road, so I must have all my wits about me.

Our destination is the Ambassador's Motel in downtown Hamilton, where the university has booked us in for six weeks while we find somewhere more permanent to live. We have special permission for Zebedee to stay with us. New Zealanders love farm dogs, but pet dogs aren't allowed in restaurants, cafes, hotels or motels, so we are very lucky.

As soon as we get to the motel, we shower and relax before heading to the supermarket, a vast Pak'nSave on the opposite side of the highway. In our accommodation, we have a fridge, oven, pots, pans, and utensils—all the essentials for self-catering. On our first night, we knock out a meal of fresh tortellini bought from the supermarket and serve it with a salad.

I'm exhausted but can't sleep, as the motel is on the main road where boy racers tune their cars to see whose can make the loudest engine noise. Not every night, I'm told. I'm hoping I'll get used to the traffic noise.

I'm up early. The car hire place is a good walk away. I collect the car at 10am and set off for Auckland. It's an automatic. My left foot is only for tapping along to the music on the radio.

As I'm driving, a wave of jetlag washes over me. Now is not the time for an out-of-body experience, I berate myself. And I've passed both Ngaruawahia and Huntly, the only towns on the route where I could pull over. Stopping on the side of the road is out of the question, as there's no hard shoulder. I sing the chorus of the Bee Gees' *Stayin' Alive* and tap my left foot.

The airport is south of the city, so it only takes me an hour to get there. I follow the signs for international cargo. When I arrive, I show my paperwork at the cargo reception centre. A customs officer checks it. I'm then passed to another official who ticks various boxes and tells me to wait.

The next moment, a forklift truck zooms out of the

restricted area, holding a wooden crate swinging in the air. I am open-mouthed. What does the operator think is in there?

'Hey,' I shout. 'She's a live animal. Be careful.' The apparatchik turns his back on me. The forklift driver hasn't heard either as he lowers his load and puts it on the ground.

'Zebedee, I promise we'll have you out of there in a jiffy.' I step forward to comfort her, but the jobsworth shouts at me.

'Stop, you can't cross that line,' he says, pointing to the customs area.

'She's been in the crate for over 24 hours, and you're treating her like a piece of meat. The paperwork doesn't even say that it's a live dog I'm collecting.'

The officer ignores me again, then prises open the crate and out walks our darling dog, looking dazed and confused, but so happy to see me.

'Thank you,' I say to the official, clipping on Zebedee's lead. I'm so glad to be walking out of there.

I spot a patch of grass outside the building. Zebedee rubs her fur on it and rolls, paws waving in the air. We go to the car, where I get her water bowl and food. She's had no food since she left England and wolfs down her meal. We walk so she can stretch her legs and do what a dog has to do before we head off in the car back to Hamilton.

I don't have a dog harness, so I push the passenger seat back and put her blanket in the footwell. She climbs on top. It will have to do as a temporary fix. I'm alert on the drive with my precious cargo on board.

We have a family reunion and show Zebedee her home from home for the next six weeks. The first thing we do is take her for a walk along the banks of the Waikato River. She pulls on the lead, trying to get to the water. The river is at least 30 metres wide at this point and fast-flowing, so we keep walking.

We walk for about half an hour towards an area with a bit of a beach, flat access and a pool, away from the strong currents.

'What do you think?' I say.

'If we let her play at the edge, it should be okay. We can throw the ball close to the shoreline,' BB Lookalike says. We unclip the lead and she splashes in the shallows, relishing her freedom. She comes out, shaking her fur all over us.

We do this walk most days, alternating between turning left at the motel and turning right. If we go left, the river becomes broader, and the current is too strong for a dog to swim against.

It doesn't take long for Zebedee to befriend other dogs. Our social life, though, takes a little longer to establish. But at the end of the first week, we are invited to a welcome dinner with senior faculty members and their partners. I sit opposite a British academic from the English department.

'What New Zealand literature do you recommend I read? I've been out of the country for a while and need to catch up.'

She looks at me as if I've asked the world's most stupid question. 'None. There are no New Zealand writers worth reading.'

Our host is a Kiwi, what a dumb comment.

'I did a New Zealand literature paper for my first degree and loved it,' I say, reeling off all the authors I'd read on the course, Katherine Mansfield included. I don't wait to find out if Mrs Only British Writers Count approves of Mansfield as I start conversing with the guest to my left, who I think is her husband.

The only other Brits we encounter with similar colonial attitudes are an elderly couple we fall into conversation with while out walking Zebedee on the racecourse.

'How long have you been here?' BB Lookalike says.

'Thirty years. It's not the same as when we first came here,' the man volunteers.

'What's gone wrong?'

The couple look at each other, shaking their heads.

'There are too many brown people now,' the woman says. I clip the lead on Zebedee, hoping to hurry away before she can say anything more. BB Lookalike is too polite to even flinch. 'We're thinking about going back to England,' she adds.

'Where are you from, then?' he says.

'Bradford,' the woman replies.

'You'll love it there now,' he says without missing a beat.

'I wonder when they were last there,' I say, as we walk away.

Long enough not to realise that it's become one of the most multicultural cities in England.

Fortunately, the other expats we meet are the complete opposite of those miserable Brits.

We throw ourselves into getting settled as soon as we can. We have six weeks to find a house to buy, but compared with England, it's a decent amount of time. In New Zealand, property can be bought and sold in days rather than weeks. Each transaction is independent of others, so there's no chain of buyers and sellers.

When we were trying to buy our first place together in London, someone further up the chain pulled out a day before the exchange of contracts. The person we hoped to buy from had nowhere to move to, and so they too pulled out. We had to start our property search all over again, and we were left out-of-pocket because we had already paid for a survey and other administration fees on a flat which was no longer for sale.

The houses I'm keen on in Hamilton line the river and are close to the town centre. They have three bedrooms and come with small gardens. BB Lookalike prefers bigger houses on larger blocks, but they are in suburbia, which I'm not so keen on. As we always take turns choosing places to live, and our home in West Kirby was my pick, I let him select our Hamilton house.

Our ambitions are modest. We want somewhere ready to move into so we can get on with living. The pressure here is mitigated because there is no stamp duty in New Zealand, so if we make a mistake and buy the wrong house, it's not the end of the world as we can easily sell it.

BB Lookalike picks a three-bedroom brick-and-tile house in Chedworth because of the wild garden out the back. Built in the 1970s, it has matching décor, a front garden, wooden decking, and a stand of native bush leading down to a flowing stream, known here as a gully. It's within walking distance of a small mall with a handy supermarket, dry cleaners, shoe repair, and other necessary shops. There are dog walks nearby, but as the area is on the outskirts of town, I fear more houses will be built on the remaining land where I plan to walk Zebedee.

It is on one of my dog walks from the motel, prior to moving to our more permanent home, that I first meet Rhonda. One afternoon, beside the Waikato River, Zebedee rushes up to a woman with a spaniel and mouths her hand.

'Ouch,' she says, pulling her hand away. 'Your dog bit me.'

'I'm so sorry. She's never done this before. Let me look. Do you need to go to the GP?'

The woman doesn't answer.

'You ought to take her to dog training,' the woman says eventually.

We did six weeks with that army battleaxe, who squirted Zebedee with a water pistol every time she did something wrong. The poor dog was terrified of her.

'I could press charges.'

Press charges?

Before I can say anything, she hands me her card. I glance at it. It says solicitor and the name of the firm.

Zebedee, you've only gone and bitten a lawyer. How am I going to get out of this one?

And then it comes to me. 'We're buying a house. Do you do conveyancing?' I say, pretending to ignore the threat of litigation.

'Yes, I do,' she says, now all smiles, fishing another business card out of her bag.

Did she forget she already gave me her card a moment ago, when she was planning to sue me?

'Call me, and we'll arrange a meeting.'

I read the name on the card. 'Thank you, Rhonda, I will.' I walk away, a spring in my step, Zebedee trotting alongside me. I can't be cross with her. Labradors use their mouths to greet people and and maybe in all the excitement, a tooth came into contact with Rhonda's hand by mistake.

When I return to the motel, I look up the firm. It's the biggest in town and certainly not the cheapest, but as this is our first house purchase in New Zealand, we want to get it right.

Later on, Rhonda and I talk on the phone.

'Find the house, then we can go through the clauses we need to add to the contract,' she advises me.

Isn't it funny, now I'm a client of her fancy law firm which charges by the quarter hour, the threat of "pressing charges" has disappeared?

The cleaners at the motel love Zebedee, and she loves them. She greets them enthusiastically every day as they come to rid our room of black dog hair.

One morning, she's sick all over the carpet, and they catch me cleaning up.

'Sorry about this, but my husband ate something which didn't agree with him,' I lie. 'He's made a bit of a mess.' They nod sympathetically, and pour some carpet cleaner onto the stain. BB Lookalike is at work, so is none the wiser about this slur against his character.

After six weeks, despite the friendly ladies, we are ready to move out of the motel. Over at our new house, we have mellifluous tuis and other native birds. The wildlife we're not so keen on are the carnivorous mosquitos. They bite humans (and dogs) day and night, especially when we're foolish enough to sit on the deck on summer evenings.

Once we've moved in and I have a desk to work at, I get back to my writing projects. I'm working alongside a director on a film adaptation of a New Zealand novel. Before I can write the screenplay, I need to secure the rights to the book. The author lives in Auckland and we arrange to meet. He is amenable to us optioning the novel and the director's agent drafts the contract.

After signing an option agreement, I work through the novel, listing the actions in the order they occur. I'm struck by how much the story jumps from one time frame to another. Then, I take all these events and put them into chronological order. From these, I select the major plot points and work them into the spine of the screenplay story, where one scene leads to another in a cause-and-effect trajectory.

It takes me a month, after which I re-read the novel. Then comes the tricky bit, as it's time to set aside the novel and let go of the subplots and minor characters I can't cram into a 90-minute screenplay. From my own notes, I lay out the theme, one of which is that in order to live in the present, you must let go of the past. As long as I'm true to the book's theme, it doesn't matter how many story threads and bit-part characters I remove. Or at least that's the theory.

I devour every article I can lay my hands on, written by authors who adapted their own novels for the screen, including Jeanette Winterson, author of *Oranges are Not the Only Fruit*, who uses the following analogy in an interview:

"A woman falls in love with a vase in an art gallery and tells the sculptor how much she admires the work, its shape, colour and glaze. As the woman goes to pay, she tells the sculptor, 'Your work is unique. Could you smash it up and make six cups and saucers?'"

I keep thinking of Winterson's analogy as I work on smashing up the novel and trying to do justice to it differently as I write my first draft. Six months in, I am satisfied it's ready to send to the script editor. I busy myself with preparing teaching materials for the undergraduate screenwriting course I've been asked to teach on, while waiting for my script feedback.

Then at a party, a man turns to me and asks, ' What do you do?'

'I'm a writer.'

'But what do you *really* do?'

In the moment, I freeze. All I want to do is get out of there, fast.

'It was great chatting,' I gabble. 'If you'll excuse me, I'm off to get a top-up.'

As he turns away and moves on to the next guest, I empty my glass.

Small town. Small minds. But why do I care what some no-mark thinks?

Later, I recount the conversation at the party to BB Lookalike and announce matter-of-factly, 'I don't think I'll thrive here.'

I'm making this all about me. I'll be turning BB Lookalike's life upside down if I do what I think I must do. Which is to sell up in Hamilton and move to Auckland, the big city up the road. Where my friends live and there's a creative community to hang out with. And when I meet a random stranger and tell them what I do, they might believe me.

This setback doesn't come close to living in London on two freelance salaries, paying a crippling interest rate of 17%, or coping with grief from recent deaths in both our families. The only drama in our lives now is on screen or at the theatre.

BB Lookalike agrees if I can make a move to Auckland work, we'll do whatever it takes.

5

One Week to Sell a House

Armed with a paper map of Auckland, I draw a big circle around the central city. The waterfront suburbs appeal, but can we afford them? I go online and search for properties from Parnell to St Heliers, but nothing beats a visit to get the feel of a place.

On a Saturday morning, I get up early and am on State Highway 1 by 7.30am, leaving Zebedee with BB Lookalike. There's very little traffic and I make it to Auckland in an hour. Waitemata Harbour sparkles in the summer sunshine to my left as I drive along Tamaki Drive to St Heliers, which has one main street, a cluster of estate agents, a post office, a chemist and a handful of restaurants and cafes. Grabbing the free property listings paper, I sit down with a coffee and glance through it, before hopping back into the car. I drive up a slope, turn right in Kohimarama, and head down the hill. I spot an estate agent's flag fluttering in the breeze and the words "Open for Inspection" on an advertising board.

I pull up. The house is a white wooden villa raised

above the ground, with moss-green window frames and a veranda at the front.

The front door is wide open. Through the hallway, the leafy back garden is visible, drawing me in. I cross the street, and the agent comes out, about to close the door behind her. She sees me, no doubt reading my body language, and quick as a flash, welcomes me into the house. I race up the three wooden steps leading to the front door.

We start in the first room on the left, the sitting room.

'The house was built in 1901. It's one of three wooden villas moved to the road.'

I'm too busy oohing and aahing over the ornate decorative carved features everywhere I look, including on the ceiling, to pay too much attention to her words. The next room we walk into is almost identical; only it's set up as a dining room. I glance at the wooden sash windows, which are a feature of every room I've seen so far.

We move on to the family bathroom. It too has ornate decorative features and a soaring carved ceiling. And, there's a claw-foot bath.

At the rear of the house is an open-plan wooden kitchen, which is double-aspect with the back door leading off to the deck area. It's spacious and light-filled, but clearly an extension, as cork tiles are on the floor rather than kauri floorboards. Despite it not being part of the original house, I can imagine cooking in it.

The main bedroom leads straight off the kitchen, which is odd. Still, it has to go somewhere. It has a built-in wardrobe in one corner and a tiny windowless "en suite" bathroom with a washbasin, loo, and shower in the other.

Is this even legal? I won't be locking the door in here. At least there's an extractor fan.

This room brings me back down to earth. We're going

to be spending money on this house, no matter what price we get it for. This doesn't put me off. I reel off a mental list of all the houses and flats I've owned, either jointly with BB Lookalike or on my own, and every single one has needed work.

'How much do they want for it?' I ask the agent.

'Ballpark $500k should do it,' she says.

'Will they take a longish settlement?'

'I can't promise, but they aren't in a hurry as they haven't found anywhere else to buy.'

I thank the agent, take a leaflet and walk out of there, feigning nonchalance, trying to keep the adrenaline rush under control. As I get back into the car, the first person I call is Rhonda.

'Is it possible to buy a house in New Zealand without selling the first one?'

'Provided you have enough for the deposit, which you can negotiate down to five per cent. You get a mortgage with a different bank. It's better to sell first, but if you can't, you can apply for a bridging loan.'

'Right, thanks so much. I've found a house in Auckland I want to buy. And I'd like you to do the conveyancing.'

'Sure, I'd love to.'

'I'll be in touch.'

I call BB Lookalike and tell him I want to make an offer on a house he has yet to see.

'I'm on my way home, but I'll call the agent and arrange for us to meet her tomorrow. We can time it so any written offer will go through on Monday, and by then, we'll be getting the Hamilton house listed for sale.'

I swear I can hear him thinking.

'Okaay, let's look at it together, and then decide.'

If it was me, I'd think I was mad, too.

It takes me over an hour to get back to Hamilton. As

soon as I'm home, I call the agent who sold us the Chedworth house.

'Hi, Katrina, we want to sell as we're buying in Auckland. Any chance you could be here first thing on Monday morning, give us a valuation, and tell us what we need to do to spruce it up for a quick sale?'

'Sure. I have a meeting at 10.15am, so how about I see you at 8.30? It's a rising market, so you might be surprised by the increase in value. But I'll be sorry to see you go.'

'Thank you so much. Let's have a coffee sometime and I'll fill you in on what's been going on. See you Monday.'

On Sunday morning, BB Lookalike, the dog, and I drive to Kohimarama. The moment they clap eyes on the beach, it is love at first sight. It's a lovely swimming beach with golden sand and a view out towards Rangitoto Island. Pohutukawa trees, coming into crimson bloom, dot the foreshore. Zebedee can barely contain her excitement as she can smell the sea and is desperate to swim, but dogs are banned during the summer.

I time the walk on the way to the house, which takes us ten minutes. We walk past the beachside cafe, the bottle shop and the fish and chip shop.

'What do you reckon?' I say.

'Pretty impressive,' BB Lookalike replies.

As we walk up the hill, I spot Valerie—the agent. At least, I spot her car. I wait outside with Zebedee while BB Lookalike gets the tour. He walks out of the house with a grin.

'Okay, shall we go for it?' I say.

'Yes.'

'The agent says we can ask for a long settlement as the

vendors need to find somewhere to move to. If we ask for two months' grace, we'll have sold the Hamilton house by then. Rhonda says it's doable. Katrina says the timing should help us as prices have gone up.'

In the UK, you can make a verbal and a written offer on a property, but they mean nothing, as you can pull out at any time. Only after the exchange of contracts, which can take months, is there any financial commitment. In New Zealand, you go from zero to sixty in one go, exchanging contracts once the written offer is accepted. You can add a few clauses and make the offer subject to various conditions, which I plan to do. Still, we must pay a deposit once those conditions are fulfilled.

'I'll make the offer subject to finance and a mortgage valuation, and put in the offer price of $500,000. So, at least we have wriggle room.'

'You know how this works, and I don't.'

'Let's see what happens, shall we?' I say, taking a deep breath as I hand Zebedee over to BB Lookalike. I walk up the steps and into the house, glancing at the ornate sitting room and dining room as I make my way to the kitchen, where Valerie is waiting with the contract. I read it through, add the two conditions, and sign my name. Then I walk out to the front garden, grab the dog lead, and swap places with BB Lookalike who is next to sign.

When we are done, Valerie comes outside to join us.

'I'll be taking the contract to the vendors later this afternoon, and I should have an answer for you this evening,' she says. 'Leave it with me.'

'We should be home by four,' I reply.

On the drive home, I can think of nothing but the house. Still, I must keep my eyes on the road, as there are some sharp bends. Close to the Waikato River near Ngaruawahia is one where there have been dozens of accidents.

The Accidental Plus One

According to Maori legend, here lurks a taniwha, a ferocious water spirit. I slow down as I reach the corner. Taniwha or not, the camber is very uneven, and my "hairdresser's four-wheel drive" (a Daihatsu Terios) seems unstable on its surface. A new car right now is low on the list of priorities when we could be stuck with two houses and a bridging loan.

We get the call later in the day to say we have a deal. I don't sleep a wink that night, and 8.30 Monday morning can't come soon enough. Katrina appraises the house and garden from the outside and I follow her, taking notes.

'It needs street appeal. A couple of plants in big pots should do the trick. When buyers do a drive-by, they'll stop to look. And some greenery in the front garden to freshen it up. And a coat of paint for the front door.' She also suggests we paint and refresh the bathroom. 'If you need some help, call this guy,' she says, handing me the card of a handyman. 'I'll start the paperwork now. If you get the work done by the end of the week, we can get it photographed on Friday and have the poster and the listing up in a week's time.'

I'm on the phone with Katrina's tradie before her car has even disappeared from view and arrange for him to visit right away to inspect the job. He gives me a quote on the spot, and I accept. BB Lookalike can help in the evenings after work, but as time is tight, I make a start by driving to the nearest garden centre to choose the plants. The pots are too heavy to load in my vehicle, so the centre offers delivery and I add half a dozen bags of compost and mulch to the order.

We get the work done in three days, and I spend Thursday running around, tidying up for the photographer. We work from room to room, moving lights, plumping cushions, and setting a bowl of lemons on the benchtop until we get the right look.

The following Monday, Katrina brings a select group of interested clients for a viewing, while Zebedee and I walk along the Waikato River near the Ambassador's Motel. We even pop in to see the room ladies who make a big fuss of her.

Katrina calls me back right after the viewing. 'Solid house in a great school zone, easy care garden, in move-in condition. Both clients were interested, one more so. And there's an Open this Wednesday from 5.30 to 6pm.'

On Friday evening at six, Katrina comes to the house with a written offer. We'll break even when we take into consideration her well-deserved commission, plus the cost of advertising and our moving costs. We countersign the offer, and it's a done deal. BB Lookalike runs across to the supermarket and comes back with a bottle of Deutz Marlborough fizz. I still can't believe my luck. This could have gone so wrong.

We clink glasses.

'Cheers to everyone. We did it.'

I call our lawyer. 'We sold the Hamilton house,' I tell Rhonda. 'So we won't need a bridging loan after all.'

For the first time in nearly two weeks, I sleep through the night.

6

Feng Shui and Double Death

One of the few sensible things I did when I started working in England in my mid-twenties was to take advantage of the property boom. Lenders were falling over themselves to sell mortgages as it was the height of the *Wall Street* Gordon Gekko "greed is good" era. And red braces were everywhere in the City of London financial district.

As my father died when I was a teenager and Mum barely had enough to live on, I was never going to have a bank of Mum and Dad. Yet I was desperate to work in the creative industries, even though there was no guarantee I'd find regular employment. So, when a film director who fled Hollywood for London during the McCarthyism "Red Scare" era offered me investment advice, I paid close attention.

'The best way to go broke is the movie business, kid. Buy property.'

So I did.

I bought my first house with a friend, but the friendship soured when I moved in with BB Lookalike. We had both been too young to consider the consequences before buying if things went wrong between us and learnt the hard way. We had to sell up but made enough profit to have a deposit each for our next home purchases.

I've been lucky, I've always sold on a rising market. The Hamilton house is the first property I've bought which merely broke even.

The first summer in Kohimarama is unforgettable. We pinch ourselves.

We put our own stamp on the place—painting the dining room a deep red and the sitting room a rich burnt orange. A new fireplace, gas fire and bespoke shelves give the room a cosy feel. The work costs more than we budget for, but doesn't it always?

Once the summer is over and teaching resumes, our routine goes like this: BB Lookalike becomes a weekly commuter, with me dropping him off at the coach station on Monday morning and picking him up again on Thursday night. He has a flat share in Hamilton with friends, and hasn't ever complained about the inconvenience I'm putting him through.

As summer turns to autumn and the temperatures drop, we wake up one morning to condensation. I wipe the single-glazed sash windows and recall all the damp student houses I lived in while at university. In one, I lay in bed at night listening to a wet tree fern slap, slap, slapping against my window in a winter storm. I'm in no hurry to revisit those days.

The coldest (and dampest) room is the spare room at the front, across the hall from the sitting room. It feels colder in here than it does outside. And it doesn't help there's no heating, apart from a portable electric plug-in. Central heating, known as hydronic heating, is expensive and not something we can afford to put in right now.

In winter, I'm mopping the windows for the umpteenth time, when I glance down at the floorboards. There are gaps between every single one. And as I look closer, to my horror, I spy the earth a foot below.

Then it hits me.

No wonder it's so cold. The house has no foundations.

On its original site, it might have done, but not since it was relocated from Devonport to Kohimarama. Valerie the agent told me the house had been moved, but I didn't know then what the pitfalls are with relocated houses. Instead of sitting on a concrete base, it is elevated, and the floors are nothing more than floorboards plonked on top of a raised platform. The house has zero insulation because of its age, and the single-glazed windows don't help either.

I'm too frightened to face facts and work out how much it will cost to fix this, so I take the coward's way out and find an affordable sticking-plaster solution in the form of a dehumidifier. Every day, I empty the water bucket—sometimes twice a day if it rains. Owning a wooden house is almost as labour intensive and costly as owning a wooden boat.

The cost of the house repairs is mounting and I need a more reliable income than freelance writing. I answer an ad in the *New Zealand Herald* for a company based in Wellington needing Auckland-based relocation consultants. Besides IT and customer service skills, the applicant needs a clean driving licence with no endorsements and a four-door saloon car no more than five years old. My recently acquired four-year-old VW Golf qualifies.

Phew! But customer service experience?

I downplayed my television production experience on the application form, fearing the company would think I was overqualified. As I spent much of my time schmoozing actors, agents and production crew, many of whom were entitled and demanding, my skill is handling tricky customers. And as for relocation, I could write the handbook. Born into a family of expats, I pinged backwards and forwards between Malaysia and England as a young child, then we emigrated to New Zealand when I was eight. As soon as I graduated from university, I fled Wellington for Sydney, then London, Liverpool, Hamilton and now Auckland.

I fly through the interview and am signed up on the spot. Jenny, my new boss, who is pleasant enough, is based in the capital, so won't be micro-managing what I do up here in Auckland. My first assignment is a family from Bedfordshire who fell in love with New Zealand on holiday. Mark, the husband, accepted a job offer from a supermarket chain here to run customer experience after being headhunted from one of the UK's household food brands.

Finding someone a place to live is far less stressful than scouting filming locations. I'm not at the mercy of a director's ego, which is a relief, as I get the job done in a few days and can submit my invoice. As soon as I get paid, I plough the money back into the house as we are knee-deep in renovations, constructing a new deck, converting the garage and turning it into a home office for BB Lookalike.

I pick up Kulap and Somchai, a young couple from Bangkok, from their short-term apartment in town. They're after a three-bedroom property to rent and have a maximum budget of $550 per week, which won't be enough to get them close to the Central Business District (CBD). I suggest focusing on the South Eastern suburbs, nearer the airport.

The Accidental Plus One

When they filled in their relocation form, their preference was a modern townhouse. They'll consider an apartment if it has a balcony and parking onsite, but they aren't interested in "old" properties. I make a guess at what they consider to be old and choose not to show them anything built earlier than 1980.

The South Eastern suburbs were farmland until the 1950s and have sprung up since then, with in-fill housing blending into a mass of single dwellings. As the housing stock is more recent than central Auckland, there's a good chance I'll find what Kulap and Somchai are looking for.

We view a contemporary two-bedroom townhouse in Golflands with neutral decor, a decent-sized kitchen, a private courtyard and a single garage. As we stand outside, I talk up the location—the next-door suburb to Botany Downs and all the shops, which Kulap loved when I first took her there. But this is a very different Kulap from the one who'd been so enthusiastic an hour before.

'Is everything okay?' I ask. Kulap shakes her head and looks downcast, while Somchai shifts from foot to foot.

Have they had a row? Is there something wrong back at home in Thailand?

I look again at the house. It's painted white, two-storey, and in a complex. There is nothing offensive about it, and on paper, it ticks all their boxes.

'Do you not want to look at it?'

'We can't,' Kulap says, pointing to the house number. It is thirteen.

Unlucky for some, clearly.

'We don't have this number in our country,' she can't even bring herself to say the word. 'We call it twelve A.'

'I'm so sorry, Kulap. I didn't realise.'

'It's very unlucky in Thai culture. It means double death,' Kulap says.

This one could have gone better.

A car pulls up and the agent, who is all smiles, gets out. I walk over to her.

I introduce myself. 'My apologies, but my Thai clients find the number thirteen so unlucky, they refuse to even look at it. I only just found this out.'

'Oh, no worries. It happens a lot down here,' she says. 'It's often about Feng Shui.'

I need this agent on my side. We are planning to see another couple of properties together, and we look down the list.

'Rather than waste your time, let me ask them if any other numbers are bad luck, and I'll be right back.'

Kulap puts me straight. I dash back to the agent.

'Number seven is bad too,' I say.

'My next two are numbers ten and nine,' the agent replies.

'Fantastic. Shall we follow you?'

I walk back to Kulap and Somchai. 'The good news is the agent has two places for us to see. Why don't you two get yourselves a coffee while I make a call?' I say, stalling for time. I head back to my car and phone the next agent we are due to meet to cancel as her property is a seven. Then I dash back to the coffee shop.

'Thank you,' Somchai says. 'We don't mean to cause any trouble.'

'Don't worry at all,' I say as we head off to view the number ten, an apartment in a low-rise complex built over several shops. The downside is it's on a busy road, although the two bedrooms are at the back of the apartment, away from street noise. The kitchen is compact and is part of the living area. There is a separate laundry area (a cupboard) for a washing machine and dryer, and the apartment has a balcony. Because it's in Howick, it's more expensive than the Double Death townhouse.

The second agent, who had the number seven, calls me as we return to the car.

'Do you know what the luckiest number is in Thai culture?'

Why didn't I think of this?

I turn to Kulap and Somchai.

'What's your favourite house number?'

'Number nine,' Kulap and Somchai say in unison.

Yes!

'I have some good news. The next property this agent will show us is a nine.'

'Can we move in?' Somchai asks.

Sight unseen?

'Let me call the second agent back to see if she has a nine in one of her listings.'

'I have everything but,' the agent says with a groan as I deliver the news.

'Sorry to make your life difficult.'

I turn off my phone and follow the first agent. As soon as we are outside the property, Kulap and Somchai are beaming.

'We'll take it,' Kulap says.

'Don't you want to see inside first?'

They shake their heads in unison.

'What about measuring up for furniture?' I suggest, grabbing my metal tape measure from my bag.

'Good idea,' Somchai says. While they measure up, I pull the agent to one side.

'As far as they're concerned, they've already moved in,' I say.

Luckily, this property is another townhouse, but this time right in the middle of Botany Downs. We speed back to the agent's office. After a couple of reference checks, she accepts Kulap and Somchai's application.

As I drive them back to their short-term accommodation in the city, I congratulate myself on going from the depths of Double Death to Absolute Good Fortune in one afternoon.

7

Living With the Mob

Scott has moved from Sydney with a global sportswear company and wants to rent a two-bedroom apartment not far from the city. He asks to be near bars and restaurants—close to the action, but not too close, as he doesn't want noise at night. As a result, the CBD is a no-go, unless the building has excellent soundproofing. Downtown Auckland has a similar problem to Hamilton with boy racers, known as "hoons," roaring up and down in their customised cars at night, in and out of the city.

I send him details of half a dozen rental properties with potential for us to view together. He has asked for an apartment with air conditioning, in a modern block. But air con isn't standard in Auckland properties as it doesn't get as hot as Sydney in summer, and it's a shame to make it a deal breaker. He gets back to me and says he'd prefer it, but it isn't going to stop him looking at places without it.

We start in Parnell, to the east of the CBD. The suburb commands a premium because it's so close to the city, so unless he ups his budget, the places within his price range will be too small and boxy. Then, we move on to an older-style apartment in Eden Terrace, between the CBD and Mount Eden. This one is too old-fashioned for his tastes, as the fit-out is dated. We are in and out in fewer than two minutes.

As I've run out of listings, I ask if he'd consider Mount Eden, which backs onto Eden Terrace.

'Come on, I'll show you,' I say. I drive him up and down the cafe strip on Mount Eden Road, and as we are returning to town, he says he'd be happy to live there. It has the right vibe, and it is still close to town.

I spend the evening trawling through real estate agents' websites, but now I've expanded the search, other properties turn up. As the housing stock is fairly old in Mount Eden, much of it consists of single-dwelling houses or large houses sub-divided into apartments.

Bingo!

I find the perfect place for him, but I don't want to get his hopes up in case it's already gone. I call the agent the following day, and to my surprise, she tells me it is still available.

'When can we see it?' I ask.

'Anytime you want.'

I message Scott and send him through the details. He's keen and says he'll meet me there to see it at lunchtime. I call the agent and set a time for 12.30pm.

When I don't know an area well, I go the day before to check it out or, like today, get there early. I park, then walk up and down the leafy, well-kept street full of expensive-looking houses. A man in his mid-sixties walking a Jack Russell comes towards me. I stop to pat his dog, who ignores me.

'How is it living here?' I ask the man.

'Safe,' he says with a knowing smile. This seems to be an in-joke, but one I'm not privy to.

'See the house across the street with the schist wall?' He nods towards a big detached house, surrounded by an expensive-looking stone fence. 'No one is stupid enough to steal from you in this street.'

'Really?'

'Any idea who lives there?'

I shake my head.

'It's the headquarters of the Mongrel Mob.'

Oh $@!£, only the most dangerous motorcycle gang in the country.

'Thanks for giving me the lowdown. I'm about to show an apartment on this street to a client.' I pat his dog again while I figure out what to do next.

'I've lived here 20 years and have had no problems. Neighbours closer to them complain about the chemical smells coming from the back of the house, and a few cars come and go in the middle of the night. But nothing serious.'

He's doing a good job selling the area. Does he own the apartment we're about to view?

While we're talking, Scott pulls up in his car. I walk over, trying to keep my composure. I don't want to ambush him, but I don't want to waste his time either.

'I've been chatting to a local who lives along the street, and he's told me you'd never get broken into round here, as the house with the fancy fence is a gang headquarters.'

He looks at the house, then the street, weighing them up before turning to me.

'I'm okay with it. If the apartment is right, it won't put me off.'

'You're sure?' He nods. 'Let's walk past first,' I say, crossing the road. 'The neighbour thinks they have a lab out the back.'

I don't think he means the canine variety, one of whom is waiting for me back home.

I inhale, then wish I hadn't as an overpowering smell of ammonia assails my senses. I try not to swallow.

'They're cooking something in there, for sure,' I say.

'Yep, smells of meth,' Scott says. I glance at the house as we go past, but the wall is too high to look over. I don't want to peer too closely in case there's a hidden security camera. If Scott's prepared to live here, knowing what his neighbours are up to, then I'm prepared to show him the apartment.

How am I going to explain this one to my boss?

But let's not get ahead of ourselves yet. Scott might not even want the apartment.

The real estate agent is waiting for us as we walk in. The place has white walls, grey carpet, a modern kitchen, two equal-sized bedrooms and the all-important reverse-cycle air-conditioning units. Scott gives me the thumbs up.

'I'll take it,' he says.

'Can we sort the lease out before Scott returns to work?' I ask the agent. *Before he changes his mind*, goes unsaid.

'Sure,' the agent says, 'my office is a ten-minute walk from here.'

'May we leave the cars here and grab a lift with you? Then we can time the walk from the coffee shop on the way back.'

'Jump in.'

As we walk over to her car, Scott takes one last look at the street before joining us. The agent grabs the opportunity and turns to me.

'I won't lie. We've had problems letting this one.'

Can't imagine why.

When I get home and am ready to send in my invoice, I worry again about what to tell Jenny. Saying nothing isn't an option as it could get back to her via the company. I email her.

"Hi, Jenny, I'm not sure you know this, but Mount Eden is a very desirable place to live, but it's also home to some rather unsavoury gentlemen. When I found out a gang owns a big detached house with an expensive schist stone wall surrounding it, I was astounded. A neighbour told me nobody gets burgled around there. Scott remains undeterred, as he's keen on the apartment and the neighbourhood. Cheers, Alison."

It's an anxious wait for Jenny to get back to me.

"If Scott's fine with it, I am too," her message says.

Good for her!

Once Scott has moved in, we catch up. He tells me about a lady collecting on behalf of the Girl Guides who had knocked on the door of the gang house. A dishevelled-looking man covered in tattoos gave her $50 for two packets of Girl Guide biscuits and told her to have a nice day.

8

Going, Going, Gone

The Davis family arrived in New Zealand with nothing more than a suitcase each, leaving behind a lifetime of memories of the farm in Zimbabwe they were forced off.

In 2000, President Robert Mugabe decreed he planned to seize all land belonging to white farmers as payback for the first white settlers in the 19th century taking land from the locals without paying for it. The Davises tell me they were luckier than most. Their loyal staff had warned them trouble was brewing. Their belongings were packed and they were ready to leave at a moment's notice. But when it did all kick off, the sight of a convoy of trucks roaring down the dirt road to the farm was terrifying. Threatened by thugs armed with sticks, many of whom were battle-scarred war veterans, the family crept towards their vehicle while their staff fended off the invaders. The vigilantes attacked other farmers who refused to go, beating them, driving them out, or even murdering them.

Hilary Davis tells me snippets about what happened after they were forced off the farm. She is heartbroken their employees, who were seen to be collaborating with the enemy, were evicted, losing their livelihoods along with their employer. They were all from the countryside and experienced in farming, while the mobs were from the cities and clueless about how to look after land and livestock.

As there was no hope of finding jobs in Zimbabwe, Hilary and Darren, along with their teenage children left in search of a safe country. Once their application to emigrate to New Zealand was successful, they sold their other assets before the Zimbabwean state grabbed them and scraped together enough money to put a deposit on a home. With most overseas clients, I advise they rent for six months when they first arrive, but given Hilary and Darren's circumstances, I want to find them a permanent new home as soon as possible.

I will need to negotiate the price on their behalf. I'll have my work cut out as it's a fast-moving property market and the family has a limited budget. I select six properties, none of which have price tags attached. As first-time buyers from overseas, Hilary and Darren are surprised.

'How do we know whether we can afford the house?' Hilary asks.

'We can use the CV—the Capital Value—as a guideline, but it will depend on how many other interested buyers there are and whether the house is being sold at auction,' I say.

'I'd better not fall in love with a place that's being auctioned,' Hilary says. Which is exactly what she does. The house Hilary wants to buy is high on the ridge next to the park in Glendowie. It's a renovated 1970s house, light, airy and spacious.

'I feel safe in this area,' Hilary says. 'The home we were forced off had been in Darren's family for two generations. But we have to forget about that. This place could really be somewhere we could make a new start.'

As it's to be auctioned, we have no way of estimating how much it will go for. I leave Hilary and Darren to wander through the property, discussing what furniture they'll need to buy.

I catch up with them as they come down the stairs. But something appears off. The couple look pensive and the real estate agent is right behind them, grinning. I hadn't seen her go up with them—I never let clients loose with agents, especially clients new to the country and unfamiliar with the buying process, but there she is.

When we return to the car, Hilary takes a handkerchief out of her bag and dabs her eyes.

'You're going to be cross with me, but the agent was crafty. She asked us what we'd be prepared to pay for the property, and I told her.'

Oh no.

'I didn't tell her how much we'd be willing to stretch to, but…'

'You weren't to know,' I say.

'I feel such a fool,' Hilary says, as my phone rings. It's the agent. We haven't moved off yet, so I turn off the engine and answer it.

'Hi, Amanda.'

What's she up to?

'We've moved the auction to Thursday evening at 6pm.' I've put the phone on speaker so Darren and Hilary can hear the agent's every word.

'Why?' Darren whispers. I turn to him, shrugging my shoulders.

'The starting bid is going to be the offer your client made, $725,000.'

I turn the speaker off, saying, 'Leave it with me,' to the

couple as I step out of the car. As angry as I am with the agent's underhand tactics, I need to play along.

I know your game.

All she's done is fire me up. Whatever it takes, I will get this house for Darren and Hilary. But I need to be two jumps ahead of her.

'And are you expecting a lot of interest?'

'At least two other interested parties,' she says. 'See you on Thursday.'

'Yes, we're looking forward to it,' I say, feeling sick. I have three days. 'I'll need to get the mortgage valuer and a builder in to do a report before then, so I'll be in touch.'

'Great,' she says before cutting me off.

Maybe she's confident another buyer will offer a higher price than Darren and Hilary can pay. But shouldn't she be keeping all interested buyers happy?

I step back into the car. Darren and Hilary are comforting each other.

'There's still an excellent chance we can pull this off.'

They say nothing.

I put aside my anger at the agent and focus on Hilary and Darren. They lost everything in Zimbabwe. The way they've been treated by the agent isn't fair. New Zealand is better than this.

'We've a few things to sort before Thursday. I'll make the calls and clear it with the agent. And give you feedback as soon as I hear from the builder.'

Hilary puts her hands in the prayer position. 'Thank you.' As we drive through St Heliers and Mission Bay on the way back to town, Darren pipes up.

'If we lose this one, there'll be another one. We already won the lottery.' I glance in my rear view mirror. Darren is transfixed by the cerulean blue of the Hauraki Gulf.

You said it.

The two reports come back by Thursday morning. The bank's valuation for a mortgage is on the conservative side. Still, as the couple has a decent deposit, we have some wriggle room at the auction. At least they now have a set figure to work to. And I know what my top bid is going to be.

The builder says the property is sound for its age. It's a renovated 1970s house and needs some cosmetic updating, but otherwise, it is structurally solid.

By the time I've talked this through with Darren and Hilary, it's mid-afternoon. I keep busy for the next few hours, but can't concentrate, as I can only think about my bidding strategy.

Most auctions take place at the real estate agency's head office. But this auction is different, as it's at the house —yet another crafty ploy by the agent. Having grilled them behind my back, she must have picked up on the couple's emotional state. An on-site auction will pile the pressure on them if they don't bid high enough.

Except I'm bidding on their behalf. And as I'm spending someone else's money, I'll be super cautious.

When we arrive at the house at 5.30pm for one last inspection, there is only one other couple there. The agent stalks in on skyscraper heels, phone glued to her ear. But whoever is on the other end of the phone isn't buying whatever she's saying, as she slips it into her pocket, not making much of an effort to conceal the disappointment on her face.

We gather from ten to six in the open-plan dining/kitchen/lounge area. The agent has a colleague with her, who I assume is the auctioneer. She'd boasted about a third set of interested buyers, but there is still no sign of them. Maybe they were on the phone to her, pulling out at the last minute.

At six on the dot, the auctioneer starts his well-rehearsed spiel, which he must have done 1,000 times before. Welcoming us to the property, he goes into an over-the-top description of the house and land, full of hyperbole, making it sound as if it's a mansion fit for an oil baron. He explains vendor bids and how they will be announced. Then, he outlines how he will conduct the auction. I smile at Darren and Hilary, trying to give them confidence I don't feel.

And we're off.

'Ladies and gentlemen, let's start the bidding at $725,000.'

Ouch, it's the price Hilary told the agent.

I try not to flinch. No one says a word. 'At $725,000. Going once. Going twice.'

Still not a word until the auctioneer puts in a vendor bid for $727k.

We haven't reached the reserve, then.

Another awkward silence. And then the once, twice refrain until the other couple look at each other. Checking with the woman he's with, who nods, the man puts his hand up.

'$727,500.'

'Thank you, a bid for $727,500. Ladies and gentlemen, I don't need to tell you this house is worth much more.'

He repeats his mantra. I raise my hand.

'$728,000.'

We go backwards and forwards in increments of $500 until the agent announces at $735,000 that the house is on the market, code for the reserve price being reached. I place my bid at $736,000. The rival bidders look at each other and shake their heads.

'Going, going, gone. Sold for $736,000,' the auctioneer says, using his arm as a gavel. Darren's face is a picture and Hilary can't stop crying.

'Congratulations,' the agent says, no doubt totting up the commission she's due to earn from the sale.

Despite your best intentions to sell it to someone else for more money.

'Thank you. It's been great to work with you,' I lie, as I'm bound to cross paths with her again.

The whole family is jumping up and down with delight, and I am infected with their enthusiasm. We have a group hug.

'We did it,' I say. Against all the odds and in a booming Auckland market, I've bought Hilary and Darren the home of their dreams without blowing their budget. They still have enough left over for furniture and any emergency renovations.

As the other bidders slink away, I can't prove it, but I have doubts they were genuine as they backed out as soon as we reached the reserve. I wouldn't put it past this agent to have brought along some mates to ramp up the auction process.

9

Tulips or Neighbours?

After five years at Waikato, BB Lookalike is ready to move on to a new challenge. He is negotiating with two universities, both based overseas. Either job will entail another upheaval: one a three-hour flight across the Tasman, the other a long-haul journey back to the other side of the world.

We go together on a visit to Melbourne in October 2005 to check it out. It's not our first visit; we'd been twice before, once on the way back from Hobart, where BB Lookalike was attending a conference and again at Easter for a holiday.

BB Lookalike makes the shortlist for the job at the University of Amsterdam, which schedules the interviews across a week in early December. We've been to Amsterdam a few times, but only ever in the summer. Curious about what life is like there in the winter, I plan to accompany him. We have enough in the bank to pay for my airfare as well as a dog sitter to look after Zebedee. At least I don't have to pay for accommodation as the university is covering the cost of the hotel. While BB Lookalike is being interviewed, I plan to view houses and apartments to see if we can find somewhere dog-friendly. And I'm also longing to meet up with friends and family who are coming from the USA and the UK to join us for the weekend.

As time is tight, we fly straight through from Auckland to Amsterdam, with a plane change in Singapore. We arrive in freezing fog and gloom in a jetlagged stupor. All we want to do is crawl under the covers in our room and sleep. Our lodgings are inside a former warehouse built in the 18th century on the Prinsengracht Canal, converted to a cosy and characterful hotel. The bedroom has heavy velvet curtains, to keep out the draughts. Because it's a period building, it is only able to accommodate secondary double-glazing, which is no match for the cold North Sea winds.

We're up early the following day as BB Lookalike has to attend an Assessment Centre for a series of aptitude and psychometric tests. It's a condition of employment for anyone applying to work in the public service. It's news to us that university staff in the Netherlands are employed by the state. In all the other places we've lived, universities are privately, not publicly owned.

We finish breakfast at 7.30am in the dining room overlooking the canal, which we can't see, as it's still pitch dark out there. BB Lookalike sets off to the Central Railway Station as the Assessment Centre is in Rotterdam, a 40-minute train ride away.

I've arranged to tour some dog-friendly areas of Amsterdam with an estate agent. I slip into a yoga class at a studio around the corner from the hotel and come back for 10.30am, when the agent is waiting in her car to pick me up.

She takes me to Oost, or the city's eastern side. The apartment we look at is on the first floor of an old building in an industrial neighbourhood. It's tiny and not the least dog-friendly, as there's no sign of a dog park anywhere nearby. We move on to the next area, De Pijp, which is trendy and has a buzzing nightlife and restaurant scene, but has a distinct lack of dog-friendly walks. This time, the apartment is in a modern building, but it's still as cramped as the first. The last area we visit is Oud-West, which has a vast green space, known as the Vondelpark.

Zebedee, you'd love this.

Apartments bordering the Vondelpark and lining the canals are the most expensive real estate in Amsterdam. The apartment we look at is in an old building and is as small as the other two the agent showed me, but costs more because of the location. If we move here, we'll have to look at living further out, either in the suburbs or another town, such as Haarlem, with good train connections.

BB Lookalike arrives back at the hotel at 6pm after what sounds a total waste of time. Finding the Assessment Centre in Rotterdam was an aptitude test in itself. On leaving the train station, he had to navigate endless underpasses beneath the vast motorway system. And then he spent the day doing pointless tests, which he aced, giving the apparatchiks carrying out the tests the answers they wanted to hear.

We get ready to go out, as this evening we are having dinner with his potential new boss and his partner. We meet up at a nearby restaurant, and I'm suddenly hit by a wave of jetlag. It's an awkward meet up, as the head of the department, Werner, can't do small talk and insists on picking apart BB Lookalike's body of work.

He's turning this into a pissing competition.

Luckily, Werner's partner, a young American, is lovely. We chat away, leaving Werner to bang on about work. At the end of the evening, when we get back to the hotel, BB Lookalike and I compare notes.

'How the hell are you going to work with him? He's jealous of your intellect,' I say.

'He has his funny little ways, but I have known him for a while.'

'It's too early to decide yet, but I'm already getting bad vibes from him.'

'Let's see what next week brings when I can meet the other colleagues.'

I draw up a list of the pros and cons of living in Amsterdam. The pros are it is so easy to get to the United Kingdom, you can travel by train. And living in the centre of Europe, we'll be within easy reach of dozens of other countries. The downsides are the climate is dreadful, and of the three neighbourhoods I viewed, only one is dog-friendly. And there are so many people in the centre of town, I feel claustrophobic. If it's this busy in December, how will it be in summer?

I'd had similar misgivings ten years ago when I had to decide whether to move to Chicago for six months.

10

The Windy City

1994
While on study leave, BB Lookalike won a prestigious Rockefeller scholarship to the University of Chicago, requiring him to move to the USA for six months.

Multi-millionaire John D Rockefeller made his fortune as the boss of Standard Oil and became a philanthropist, bequeathing the university over $35 million between 1892 and 1910. Thanks to Rockefeller's generosity, Chicago became one of the world's leading research universities in 20 short years.

Winning this generous scholarship was a big deal, and I was excited for him. But there was a snag.

'You know I have no holiday entitlement for an entire year, so I can't come with you?'

'I didn't.'

'I'm on a self-employed contract, not an employee one. It's the only way I could make it work, paying the mortgage up here and rent down there.' Even if I had been an employee, there was no way my boss would have given me six months' unpaid leave. Television is far too competitive an industry, with a new cohort of eager young hopefuls coming up behind, ready to replace me. I talked to HR, but the best they could come up with was a week off unpaid in March.

'If you go on your own, you'll be able to get the new book written with no distractions.'

Even if I could have gone, there was another roadblock. The University of Chicago's main campus was in the South Side of the city in Hyde Park, a bubble of privilege surrounded by challenging neighbourhoods with high crime rates. Despite the university having one of the largest privately funded police departments in the country, even in Hyde Park, car-jackings, muggings and robberies occurred in broad daylight.

In any of the cities where I feel safe, you can be mugged if you are unlucky. A knife is the most likely weapon of choice. And while knife crime kills, the attacker can only stab one person at a time, unlike a perpetrator armed with an automatic firearm. In the USA, it's different and I wouldn't feel safe alone, particularly at night in winter when it gets dark early.

I am a walker. I prefer to walk than take a bus or a train. I do it as a form of exercise and for my mental health. I chat to people I meet. Even in the area where I rent a room in London, I feel safe walking home alone from the Tube at night as it's well lit.

'I've just found out it's a dry campus apart from one bar serving beer,' BB Lookalike said.

'A dry campus apart from beer? At a university? What horror is this? I didn't realise the Puritans went as far as the Great Lakes.'

I thought about Liverpool, a party town, where drinks after work on a Friday night had been a part of our social life since we moved there. When I started working in

London, it stopped because on Friday nights, my train didn't arrive in Liverpool until 10pm, and we went straight home. But on Saturday nights, we often headed back into town to meet friends.

If I went with BB Lookalike on this jaunt, I'd depend on him for my social life.

Instead, we leased out our flat on Merseyside and I decided I'd stay full time in London for six months while BB Lookalike was away. Because I worked in London from Monday to Friday, I was already renting a room at a friend's house during the week.

BB Lookalike found himself a room to rent near the university campus in what was supposed to be a safe neighbourhood with a landlady who was a devout Christian. His apartment overlooked a little park with a children's play area.

I flew to Chicago in March 1995 for a week. Work was reluctant to let me go and made me feel guilty about the extra burden foisted on my two production coordinators. But as we all looked out for each other, they knew I'd do the same for them.

BB Lookalike's rented room was too small for both of us, so we booked a hotel in downtown Chicago. He met me at O'Hare and we took a taxi downtown. The cab drove along the shore of Lake Michigan, a lake I couldn't even see to the other side of, so vast it was like a sea. We drove past glitzy apartment blocks overlooking the lake. This was the Chicago of Oprah Winfrey and the famous shopping street, the Magnificent Mile. I couldn't wait to explore it.

During my visit, we walked beside the Chicago River, went up the Sears Tower, visited the Art Institute of Chicago, ate out and browsed the shops. My favourite was a massive Barnes & Noble, which even had a cafe inside it with comfy sofas.

Sharon, BB Lookalike's landlady, and her friends invited us to dinner at the apartment one evening. Dinner was early, at 6pm, and we travelled on the subway at peak time, along with all the commuters. Even though we had to watch out for pickpockets, we were surrounded by others who treated this journey as routine. And when we arrived in Hyde Park, the streets were busy.

We were early.

'Can I do anything to help?'

'Sure,' Sharon said. 'How about going to the store for salad dressing?'

'You mean vinaigrette?'

Sharon shook her head. 'No, honey, I meant Paul Newman's.'

Did she really want to buy a ready-made salad dressing from a jar when it would take 30 seconds to make one?

'All I need is olive oil, lemon juice, salt and mustard.'

'Super. I think we have all those ingredients. I'd love to see it made from scratch.'

We arrived back from the supermarket armed with two bottles of white wine for the six of us. BB Lookalike and I didn't think to mention it to Sharon because in Britain, when you are invited to dinner, unless it's formal, it is customary to bring wine. I knocked out the dressing and brought it to the table, where Sharon's friends were sitting.

'Guess what? Alison makes her own salad dressing!' The guests cried "wow" and "really?"

It's only salad dressing.

As we sat there at the table, I whispered to BB Lookalike he might want to fetch the wine from the fridge. He came back clutching a bottle in each hand and started offering them to the guests. All four shook their heads and smiled.

'No thanks.'

BB Lookalike took the bottles back into the kitchen, and returned with two tumblers of wine, handing one to me. Once he'd sat down, the murmuring stopped and Sharon spoke.

'For what we are about to receive, may the Lord make us truly thankful.'

Sharon and her mates must belong to a Christian sect which bans alcohol.

And it was not the Christianity BB Lookalike and I (both lapsed Catholics) were familiar with. In our world, whether your heritage is Italian or Irish, as ours is, a drink after Mass at a meal is considered normal.

We drank a bottle of wine between us and stashed the other one to take back to our hotel. After our meal, a guest offered to drop us off at the subway in their car so we wouldn't have to walk there.

We returned to Hyde Park the next day. I mentioned to BB Lookalike I needed to find a cash machine.

'There's one right outside the apartment on the street corner, but it's too dangerous to use it.'

'Where the heck do I get money out then?'

'Either a bank or a machine inside a building with good security.'

We tried but failed to find a bank. Across the road was a big hospital.

'What about in there? No one's going to rob you in a hospital, are they?'

'We'll give it a try,' BB Lookalike said. We crossed the

road and headed for the glass doors. Behind us, sirens went off, and ambulances pulled up.

'Bloody hell, this is the way to the ER.' Any minute now, Dr Ross from the TV series would sprint along the corridor. And if I'd tried, I couldn't have picked a more inappropriate moment to ask where to find money.

'Excuse me, but can you tell me where the nearest cash machine is?' I asked a stressed-looking medic.

'Huh? I don't know what you're talking about, lady.'

What do they call it here, then?

I rattled off a few possibilities.

'Cash station?'

'No, ma'am.'

It's an ATM.

And I spotted one next to a drinks vending machine. I looked over my shoulder as I withdrew my cash. Nobody was behind me, and as far as I could tell, there was nothing suspicious about the machine, although I wouldn't know what a skimming device looked like.

Who knew getting money out of an ATM was such a mission?

We spent the afternoon on a Frank Lloyd Wright architectural bus tour, which included a visit to Robie House in Hyde Park, now part of the University of Chicago campus. Built between 1909 and 1910, it is a vast, low-level single-family home. The space here was lateral rather than vertical.

'It's so different to Europe and Britain, where houses go up, not out, because square footage is at a premium,' I said.

Robie House is one of the finest examples of the Prairie Style, which was inspired by the flat plains of the American Midwest. Land must have been cheap on the prairies, but in suburban Chicago, even in 1909, you'd still need a large sum of cash to buy a block this big.

The Accidental Plus One

Frederick C Robie was only 28 when he commissioned Wright to build his house. Although he was working in the family business, one of the country's largest distributors of automotive parts, he was a lowly Assistant Manager.

We returned to the tour bus and headed off to Oak Park, one of the swankiest neighbourhoods in Chicago. On the way, we passed the surrounding areas of Hyde Park. There were run-down tenement-style houses with peeling paint, some surrounded by chain-link fencing, interspersed with empty lots full of weeds growing out of them.

Our tour guide announced: 'Folks, we're stopping in a couple of blocks, as I want to show you a house inspired by Wright. We will get out to cross the street, but make sure you keep together as a group. And the driver will keep the engine running in case we encounter any problems.'

'It reminds me of going on safari and watching out for lions,' I whispered to BB Lookalike.

The guide was on edge, checking the coast was clear.

No wonder he's so nervous. A tour bus in a run-down neighbourhood marks us as outsiders.

We couldn't get back on the bus quick enough. Once we left the South Side, the houses looked better cared for. The closer we were to Oak Park, the bigger and ritzier the mansions. And as for the gardens—some were as big as parks.

On Friday 17 March, St Patrick's Day, the hotel staff greeted us dressed as leprechauns and offered us green cookies.

'Maybe after breakfast?' We slunk out of the dining area and went back to the room.

As we headed off for our walk, signs and notices about

street closures for Saturday's St Patrick's Day parade were everywhere.

'Tomorrow is a day for museums, don't you think?' I said.

'Good idea,' BB Lookalike said.

I stared at the Chicago River flowing underneath a bridge. It was a lurid fluorescent green.

'They dye the river?' We shook our heads.

The fuss over St Patrick's Day in Chicago was a sight to behold. There might be a big parade in Dublin, but there is no dyeing the Liffey green. The Irish don't need to. It'll already be full of green algae. How cynical we are on the other side of the Atlantic. Chicago is proud of its immigrant heritage, and if I drank Guinness, I'd have raised a glass to it.

My week in Chicago was over all too soon. It had taken me two days to forget about work, but now I couldn't think of anything else. We checked out of the hotel on Sunday morning and spent the last day in the city. My flight was the red-eye on Sunday night.

In the half-light known as the arrivals area at Heathrow at 6.30am, I gambled on a quiet day at work, as Mondays usually were. It turned out to be anything but peaceful, which is to be expected in live television. You can read all about it in my career memoir, *Misadventures in the Screen Trade*, (see the Also by section at the end of this book.)

11

On the Market

Fast forward ten years and the decision we're about to take is going to have a lasting impact on our lives and our future. My misgivings about Amsterdam differ from Chicago, but they're still to do with how we'd live. It's not dog-friendly, it's crowded and there are too many tourists. And I worry the work culture will get BB Lookalike down. His contract states he must conduct all policy and management tasks in Dutch and is expected to learn the language to a high standard.

But I'm torn, even though I can see the disadvantages. The Netherlands is so close to family and friends in England. Our reunion on the weekend in Amsterdam with loved ones was magic and underscored how much I miss them all.

On the long flight home to New Zealand, we have the chance to talk everything through. I view Amsterdam in the short-term as a stepping stone back to the UK. BB Lookalike thinks Australia offers a long-term solution with a better quality of life, but we agree the major drawback is "the tyranny of distance" (a phrase coined by historian Geoffrey Blainey).

While we wait for decisions from both universities, I have to face facts—my beloved dream home has become a liability. We could have fixed it up in our own time if BB Lookalike had been offered a job in Auckland. I fantasise about hanging onto the house and letting it, but given its age and condition, we'd be forever shelling out for repairs. The added hassle of being long-distance landlords is something we could both do without. And so, with heavy hearts, we decide the realistic option is to sell.

I call an agent from the company that sold us the house, but they decide two agents are better than one. Tweedledum and Tweedledee recommend selling by auction, although I'd prefer they put a price on the house. They recoil in horror.

'You get more at auction. A fixed price limits what you could get for it,' Tweedledee says. I interpret this to mean, 'We could get a higher commission if we sell by auction.'

'But what if it gets passed in?' I voice my concern that the bids won't meet our hopes and expectations. The agents squirm.

'We round up the interested buyers, and by the end of the day, there'll be an offer on the table.'

If I sound as if I'm an expert on buying and selling houses in New Zealand, it turns out I am. My pitch to Vacation Work, a travel publisher based in Oxford, results in a two-book deal to write guidebooks for their living and working abroad imprint. They have published a book about Australia, but New Zealand is yet to feature. My relocation experience and published newspaper articles swing it for me. The books they commission are *Buying a House in New Zealand* and the New Zealand section of *Retiring to Australia and New Zealand*.

I sign a standard seven-year book contract, which includes a publisher's advance against royalties for the first book. Since the second book will be written for a niche market, I opt for a buy-out contract for the same fee. The deadline is nine months to deliver both manuscripts. In addition, I have a monthly paid screenwriting column for the UK's most widely read magazine for writers.

Two books to write, a house to sell, plus an international move to organise. How am I going to get this done?

Tweedledum and Tweedledee send one of their minions to help us prepare the house for sale. The agent stops on the front step and surveys the book-lined hallway with distaste.

'No,' she says. 'You can't leave those there. It makes the hallway look small. I suggest you pack up all the books and put them into storage.' When I relay this to BB Lookalike, he is apoplectic.

'Most of those books are for work. I can't do my job without them.'

'We'll move the essential ones into your office and box up everything else.'

The agent tells us we need to renovate the kitchen bench tops, replace the cork floor and repaint the outside of the house. I'm reeling when I work out how much the painting is going to cost.

All the money I'll be earning from these books will be spent on doing up the house so we can sell it.

I call the builder who transformed the garage into BB Lookalike's home office. Gary makes a living building new houses and wrinkles his nose at this one. He shakes his head.

'Hey, Al, I could build you a nice new house with a double garage for half the price you'll pay to maintain this old one,' he says.

'Thanks, Gary. But then we'd have to tear down the office you built for us.'

'Then you'd have an integral double garage.'

'The people who buy it might be interested, but for now, let's do the best we can to sell it.'

'It's your money,' he says with a grin.

Despite having to project manage all the repairs, I work day and night to deliver the first manuscript to Vacation Work in the week leading up to Christmas. It's months before I can invoice, as the book will need developmental, line, and copy edits, plus a proofread. But I can send my first invoice for the advance on the second book, which will pay for the bench tops and the flooring, at least.

Once the kitchen and exterior painting is finished, I enlist the support of visiting family members, who spend hours cleaning windows, dusting and polishing until the house looks so enticing, none of us can bear the thought of having to part with it. I even buy a lottery ticket in the vain hope miracles happen and we can keep it. But reality hits once again as we dress the house for the photographs.

Then a full-colour display board goes up outside and the agents organise the first Open Home.

An Open Home is a marketing method adopted from the USA where complete strangers or, worse still, the neighbours can inspect your house. For British people, who regard their home as their castle, it would be unconscionable. The agent who runs it has to make sure nobody walks out with any of your stuff. As someone who once had their shoes stolen from under a park bench in Liverpool, I hide away all the valuables and take my laptop and phone with me during the Open.

While BB Lookalike curates a suitable music selection to play in the background, the rest of us tidy, clean and remove all the evidence a dog lives here. Once this is done, we admire the new paintwork as we stand on the front porch, ready for the agent to arrive.

'Wow! It looks great. I'm so glad we made the effort.'

And then, a small winged insect emerges from a freshly dug hole in a newly painted weatherboard.

'What the hell? It can't be a borer,' I wail.

A quick-thinking family member comes to my rescue.

'Any Tippex?' he says.

'Yep.' I look at my watch. The agent is due in five minutes. I rush inside and grab the bottle of liquid paper, and we apply it to cover up the hole. It works a treat.

After the Open Home, the agent who told us to remove all our books from the hallway turns up unannounced.

'May I come in and have a look?' she says. I don't know why she's here. 'I'll take it off your hands for you,' she offers. 'For cash. And a quick sale.'

I count to ten to keep myself from exploding.

'If I get desperate, I'll call you,' I say with a fixed grin. As the agent walks down the steps and into her car, I call to the others.

'Did you hear what she said?'

'Yes.'

'I wish I'd recorded her, she's shameless,' I say, shaking my head.

Four months after the interview at the University of Amsterdam, BB Lookalike is offered the job. The University of Melbourne's offer came through weeks earlier and, tired of waiting, BB Lookalike said yes, so he turns down Amsterdam. His would-be boss, who was insufferable at our dinner, is angry.

Once a starting date is nailed down, I contact a relocation company in Melbourne to find us a house for rent willing to take a dog. Our house sale has become more urgent as we have fewer than two months before BB Lookalike takes up his new post.

After the flying insect drama, I double-checked with the pest control company that treated the wood in our house. Our certificate was still valid and what I saw was a "one-off," they told me. I keep checking the woodwork and see no more, although I don't look too hard. We'll know for sure if it gets flagged up as an issue, if a buyer gets a builder's report. And flying insects are the least of our worries when it rains—and rains and rains. One day, water pours through the ceiling rose in the hallway onto the polished kauri floorboards. With all this wet weather, we have stationed a bucket underneath the leaky roof until we figure out how to fix it.

Our roofer tells us when all the chimneys were removed before the house was relocated, the remaining roof had to be sealed. There is a valley in the middle where the chimney was, and water collects there. Because of all this rain, it's overflowed and put pressure on the old roof, and through a tiny gap, the water has forced itself into the ceiling. We can't afford either the time or the money to replace the roof, so we do the next best thing and get it patched up.

Two weeks into the advertising campaign, we wake up one morning to see a stream of mud flowing down our sloping back garden.

'Where's it coming from?' I say.

'I don't know, but we're going to need to investigate,' BB Lookalike says.

Disasters always seem to come in threes, don't they?

'Let's do the dog walk behind the house today,' I say. We fling on clothes, grab the lead plus dog and head off.

Backing onto our back garden at the top of the hill, where once an old house stood, is now a cleared building site.

'He must have planning permission,' I say as I stare at the mud covering the site. This mud, along with any topsoil left, is flowing down the hill, through our back garden down a trench and landing on the paved area right outside BB Lookalike's brand new office.

While we are surveying the sorry mess up at the site, the owner who is working on the project turns up. We have met him once before and he admits he's responsible for the subsidence. Every time it rains, he promises to send his contractors to remove the mud and cover up the mess. And he's as good as his word.

And then, for once, luck appears to be on our side and the rain stops as abruptly as it started. The ground dries up, and fingers crossed it will stay fine until auction day.

The auction starts at 5pm, so I try to work on my second relocation book until then, but can't concentrate. As BB Lookalike and I walk upstairs into the auction room, it's cheek-by-jowl in there.

We have to sit through 20 other auctions. The last house to go up for sale before ours is a kauri villa, similar to ours. But it's on the original plot with all its original features intact, including the brick chimneys. And it's in a sought-after inner-city suburb. With four competing bidders, the auction cracks along at a pace. It sells just shy of $1 million.

I have high hopes for ours, but then the crowd melts away until it's us two, a couple in their fifties, the two agents and the auctioneer. My instinct is to dash out of the room, to be spared the humiliation of what's about to happen, but it's too late. My dismay turns to anger and I want answers from our two shifty agents who have been stringing us along when, all this time, they only had one interested party.

The auctioneer opens with a vendor bid, then there is total silence. Not one person raises their hand. I want to sink through the floor.

After the auction, we leave without saying a word to either agent. If I open my mouth, I know I'll put my foot in it.

The following day, Tweedledee rings me.

'The couple who came to the auction want another viewing.'

'The ones who didn't bid?'

'They saw it at an Open Home, but because they're British and unfamiliar with the auction system, they didn't want to bid.'

Then why did we go ahead with that charade?

'When do they want to come? Ten minutes? Let me pack up the dog and her things, and we'll leave you to it.'

Zebedee and I get into the car and sit in front of the beach at St Heliers.

'We'll miss this, won't we?' I say, giving her a hug. 'But don't worry, we'll find you another beach.' While we sit in the car waiting for the viewing to finish, I use the time to confirm all the documentation for Zebedee's relocation to Australia. We are lucky there's no quarantine between the two countries; she's up to date with all her vaccinations and is free of rabies. And what's more, it's only a three-hour flight. I've paid for a pet relocation company to do all the shipping paperwork for me, and they will even pick her up. We can all travel together on the same flight, but they'll organise the customs checks at the other end and will deliver her to our rented house as soon as these are done.

While I'm thinking about this, the agent rings me.

'I have an offer for you which you'll like.'

'I'm on my way,' I say. I spot BBLookalike, who'd nipped to the shops and pull over to collect him. Five minutes later, we arrive at the house. Tweedledee shows us the offer. It's over the auction reserve. We countersign it. Tweedledum introduces us to the delightful couple who have bought the house.

'We've sold our house in England, and it's our dream to restore an old house. I'm a structural engineer and know there's work to do here,' the husband says.

'Thank you,' I say. 'Thank you for buying it. I'm so glad it's going to be looked after.'

Imagine if Gary, the builder, had bought it, only to knock it down to build a McMansion.

12

Welcome to Australia

I walk through the now-empty house for one last time, fighting back the tears. Although I get why we must move, I wish it was Sydney we were off to, where I lived after university and my friends are based. I don't know anyone in Melbourne.

We combined a recce visit with a conference in October 2005, during a freak heatwave when the mercury hit 35C. I pinpointed a few dog-friendly areas and set off for the first in Northcote, north of the Yarra River, where some of BB Lookalike's friends live. After being overcome by the heat and the fumes, I sat down near the river and decided I'd never survive a Melbourne summer this far inland.

Friends had also recommended Williamstown to the west for its beaches and dog-friendly parks. Despite the distance from the city, it has good public transport connections. The train left Flinders Street station in downtown Melbourne and arrived 25 minutes later at the seaside. Despite the blistering hot day, there was a breeze blowing in from Port Phillip Bay.

The Accidental Plus One

When BB Lookalike arrived, we walked down towards the Yarra River and Gem Pier, and along Nelson Place, the historic cafe and restaurant precinct. By now, the temperature had climbed to 37C. In front of us was Capriccio, an Italian gelateria, which we couldn't go past. As we ate our gelatos, gazing out over the bay towards Melbourne, we looked at each other.

'I don't think we'll get better than here,' I said. And the decision was made.

Because of the dog, we negotiate with the university's HR department to trade part of our moving allowance, which includes one month in a serviced apartment, to pay a relocation consultant to find us somewhere we can move into straight away with hired furniture. Our consultant comes up trumps and finds a new 3-bedroom townhouse in Williamstown North, with polished wooden floors and a patio area. It looks fantastic in the photographs and the bonus is we will be the first tenants to live there.

At Melbourne airport, we present our passports to immigration, thinking it will be a quick check of all our documentation. Despite our New Zealand passports, which give us the right to work and live in Australia through a Trans-Tasman Travel Arrangement, we applied for and received Australian Permanent Residence with this move.

The customs officer peers at our passports and shakes his head. 'It's not normal for New Zealanders to have Australian Permanent Residence,' he says. 'I need to check with one of my colleagues.'

Five minutes later, he comes back. 'It's okay, you can go,' he says.

'Thank you,' we reply.

'That didn't go as smoothly as I was expecting, but let's grab a taxi,' I say.

'Don't expect they'll tell us what the problem was, either,' BB Lookalike says.

We join the queue for a taxi to take us to Williamstown and head off to our accommodation, where our consultant is waiting with the keys.

'I'm so sorry,' she says. 'They only finished sealing the floors today. I've had all the doors and windows open, trying to get rid of the chemical smell.'

'I love it. You've done such a great job,' I say. 'And we're so grateful.' We keep the patio doors and all the windows open until it's time to turn in, so the fumes don't knock us out. To walk into a furnished house and know we don't have to move out of it for six months is such a relief.

After a sound night's sleep, BB Lookalike wakes up, complaining a mosquito bit him in the night.

I examine his face. 'Oh yes, there it is, under your right eye.'

He goes off to the University of Melbourne for his first official day's work. But when he arrives home in the evening, I stare at him.

'You look like a hamster that took on Mike Tyson and lost.' His right eyelid is so swollen, he can't even see out of that eye. 'It was one angry mosquito. And the bite could be infected. You'd better get it looked at by a medic.'

It's six in the evening and all the GP surgeries have closed. But our relocation guidebook has emergency after-hours hospital contacts.

'There's a cottage hospital in Williamstown, near the beach, with an Accident and Emergency Unit. Let's go.'

It's so close, we can walk. A doctor sees **BB Lookalike** within half an hour and treats him with antibiotics.

'It wasn't a mosquito. It's a whitetail spider bite,' **BB Lookalike** says when his consultation has finished.

'We have a nest of dangerous spiders lurking in the patio garden of a new townhouse?'

'And all their relatives.'

When we get home, I tour the house and the patio, but find no evidence of any arachnids. The sitting and dining room floors still reek of chemicals. If industrial strength fumes didn't put the spider off, I don't know what will.

I wake up the following day, and I'm bite-free. So is the dog, as far as I can tell. **BB Lookalike** goes to work, his face still swollen and barely able to see out of one eye. At work, he tells me later, he's queuing for lunch in the canteen when he overhears a conversation.

'Have you met the new Head of Media? Nice bloke, but %^$£ is he ugly!'

This first round of antibiotics is being slow to take effect.

After a week, the spider bite is no closer to healing, and the swelling is getting worse. We return to A&E at Williamstown Hospital.

'The swelling is getting rather close to your brain,' the doctor says.

'Which I need for work,' says **BB Lookalike**, deadpan. The medic giggles.

In our first 48 hours here, BB Lookalike took on a whitetail and lost. What other toxic creatures has this country lined up for us? Welcome to Australia!

13

Underbelly

Williamstown is full of homes similar to our kauri villa in Auckland, but they're more expensive here, as we lose out converting New Zealand dollars to Australian. And we have to pay stamp duty on our purchase. I estimate the latter will be approximately $35,000—the cost of an extra bedroom. As first-time buyers in Australia with Permanent Residency, we qualify for a grant, which mitigates some of the extra costs.

Stamp duty isn't only levied on house purchases, either, I discover. I want to drive a fuel-efficient hybrid, so I find a Toyota Prius, a former government fleet car. I don't check which state government. It's a reasonable price and is being sold by a dealer in Wollongong.

Wollongong, it sounds familiar. I'm sure I've been there.

The dealer is so keen to offload this car, he offers to deliver it to my door. We seal the deal. While waiting for the money transfer to go through, I locate Wollongong on the map. Now I know why it's familiar—I've driven through it on the way to Sydney. Which is in New South

The Accidental Plus One

Wales, some 930 kilometres by road, a nine-hour drive away. It is comparable to living in Birmingham, West Midlands, England, and buying a car in John O'Groats, the northernmost tip of Scotland.

I've only gone and bought a car inter-state!

If I'd done my geography homework, I could have saved myself the $650 delivery charge and the $400 stamp duty and the cost of the Victoria number plates I have to buy.

When a flatbed truck arrives outside my door, the driver jumps out and hands me the keys. I'd better get used to driving this thing before I head off to register it and swap my New Zealand driving licence for a Victoria one. Ours is a quiet, leafy suburban street, and there's nobody about. The car is so quiet, I can't even hear the engine. When I stop at the first intersection, it cuts out. I practise parking and finding reverse, check the indicators and locate the windscreen wiper controls.

My nearest VicRoads office is in Sunshine, 13km northwest of Williamstown. I consult Melways, Melbourne's map book, before I set off. The route looks straightforward if I stick to the main roads. This is only my second time driving in Melbourne, so I'm trying to keep calm. The traffic volume is as heavy as Auckland's in rush hour. Not only are there far more trucks, but all the other vehicles are massive utes driven by men in hi-vis jackets. Sunshine is awash with warehouses, car dealerships, and endless industrial units.

What clown named this place?

You'd never get away with naming anywhere in England Sunshine, as it's tempting fate there. Or was it a marketing ploy, giving it a jolly name to cheer up the folks who have to live here? It turns out the place was named after a local employer, the farm machinery manufacturer Sunshine Harvester Works. As I drive back with my new number plates and licence, I think of Bill Withers' song *Ain't No Sunshine*.

No more Sunshine for me either, now I have wheels and can start looking for a house to buy.

I find my perfect pad in Newport. It's a former ship chandler's premises, which then became the local ice cream shop. Through a clever renovation, the owner, who is an architect, has transformed it into a three-bedroom, two-bathroom house. Original floorboards, long red velvet curtains, and a chandelier in the open-plan kitchen-diner work their magic on me. I'm drawn to old houses. I can't help myself.

The dining room faces Douglas Parade, but the internal shutters on the windows prevent anyone from looking in from the street. The kitchen is white, bespoke, and industrial, with shiny cabinetry and a massive stainless-steel table which works as a makeshift island. Above the table is a series of three white pendant lamps. Along one wall is a ton of floor-to-ceiling storage. An American fridge and an enormous detachable tap, nicknamed the "beast," set above the stone benchtop complete the look.

At the back of the house is the cosy sitting room, which opens out onto the patio area, with a built-in stone benchtop and gas barbecue. The designers have thought through every little detail, including a cleverly disguised recess area for the bins. There's even a retractable washing line. The downside is there is only a patio garden, and no grassed area for Zebedee.

Between the living room and the kitchen is a second

The Accidental Plus One

bathroom with a bath by the Italian designer Alessi, who must never have sat in it. Even I don't fancy lying down in a bath made of uncomfortable-looking mosaic tiles.

The narrowest and steepest staircase I have seen in a long time, no doubt installed 100 years ago when the house was built and there were no building regulations, leads off from the kitchen. Upstairs are three small bedrooms, two with built-in wardrobes, plus a tiny en suite shower.

BB Lookalike is underwhelmed, disliking the aspect facing towards the industrial part of the Yarra River.

'It's too far from the beach for the dog,' he says. (And for him, I suspect.) And the big drawback is a paved patio won't work for a Labrador. I point out as it's Newport, we'll be closer to the city, yet still within walking distance of Gem Pier, Nelson Place, and our favourite gelateria. And it's within our budget. But as we take turns with houses and I chose in Auckland, it's only fair BB Lookalike picks the Melbourne house.

One agent comes up with a house I reject out of hand, but BB Lookalike wants to view. It's a four-bedroom, two-bathroom townhouse in an "award-winning development."

It can't have won for the paint job or is it only me who doesn't like battleship grey and Federation red and yellow?

As we stand outside with the agent, waiting for the owners to answer the door, I notice the Venetian blinds on the window nearest the front door are closed shut.

Office blinds don't say "buy me."

All the other houses we've viewed have not only had blinds open, but lights on (an agent trick for showing off dingy rooms). Not this one.

Someone has spotted us despite the drawn blinds and they open the front door. A couple in their late-thirties usher us into an open-plan sitting room. I glance to my right. Three children, who I guess range in age from about six to twelve, sit upright on the sofa. Their eyes follow our every move like a trio of baby owls.

This is weird. Why are they home during the viewing?

'Do look around, won't you?' the woman says. I am struck by the gloom, not helped by the dark brown sideboard tucked up next to a feature wall painted hazelnut.

A feature wall? In brown? This place reminds me of a bad reality TV makeover show.

The only thing going for it is its size, almost double the square footage of the Newport ship chandler's. We could both have an office plus a guest room. And because it needs a new kitchen and some landscaping in the back garden, we could put our stamp on it.

Never in a million years did I envisage living somewhere like this, but the selling point is it looks straight out towards Port Phillip Bay. There are dog-friendly walking tracks, a bird sanctuary, and Williamstown Beach a five-minute cycle ride away. The roads on the estate have been designed to bamboozle everyone bar the locals, with confusing dead-ends and only one through road in and out. People who live down here value their privacy, the agent tells us.

'See the house down there,' he says, pointing to one with three storeys and a sea view. We nod. 'When' and he names a Greek-Australian tennis player 'comes down here to see his family, he knows he won't be stalked by the paparazzi.'

I don't think being chased by camera crews is a problem we'll have.

'Something doesn't seem right to me,' I say. 'Those kids. Why were they sitting there like that?'

'Sorry. I couldn't get the family to leave. They're very security conscious.'

'They didn't want us to view the house without them being there?'

'Yeah,' the agent says, looking down at his shoes. 'But they need to sell.'

Could their reasons for selling be one of the four Ds?

'Are they splitting up?'

'No, there's more to it.'

If they're not getting divorced and nobody's died, could it be debt or decamping?

'One is a detective, and the other is in the security service. And they have to keep moving house to protect their kids. Even if you make a lower offer, you might get it.'

BB Lookalike's ears prick up.

'Okay, we'll talk it over this evening and get back to you,' I say.

I concede there are too many downsides to the Newport place and the sort of house I want to buy is out of our price range.

'You prefer the townhouse, don't you?' I say to BB Lookalike.

'If we could get it for lower than the asking price, yes.'

'Let's give it a go.' We put in the lower written offer and the vendors accept it and countersign.

At least the money we save can offset some of the renovation costs.

We move in a month later. Once we've been in a while, I investigate the world of organised crime in Melbourne, and what I find out makes my hair stand on end.

Two rival gangs fall out over who gets to control the methamphetamine trade. And in an act of retribution, one gangster goes on a killing spree, wiping out as many members of the rival gang as he can. First arrested and convicted of murder in 2004, Carl Williams, dubbed the "baby-faced killer," confessed to another three deaths in 2007. But detectives working in the specialised unit set up to investigate believe the real number is more like ten.

And I'm guessing we went and bought a house off one of those detectives.

14

Up to the Top End

BB Lookalike and I are working out the plot of a thriller we are co-writing. We're yet to decide if we'll incorporate any of the Melbourne gangland crimes in the storyline, but as one of the subplots involves uranium mining, we take a trip to the Northern Territory during the mid-year semester break.

It's the perfect time of year as it's mid-winter in the Top End. But even in winter, the temperatures reach the mid 30s. We pull out the map and book a room at the "Croc Hotel," designed in the shape of the large reptile. As well as looking at rock art and wildlife, we plan to visit the Ranger uranium mine, inside the boundary of Kakadu National Park. We're keen to find out why the mine can operate within a UNESCO World Heritage Area, but I'm sure ERA, the mining company, will tell us on our tour.

As well as the current mine, marked on the map are abandoned uranium mines dotted throughout the Northern Territory in remote areas with difficult access. Most vehicle hire companies won't let you drive on unsealed roads, unless you pay extra for a four-wheel drive.

'I'm so sorry, but we don't have any cars left,' the Darwin-based vehicle hire rep says, looking up from her computer. 'But we can upgrade you to a four-wheel drive for the same price.'

I should be leaping over the desk by now to thank her. Instead, I pull a face and shuffle from foot to foot in embarrassed silence.

I turn to my co-writer. 'What do you think? It's not very eco,' I stage whisper. The rep taps away on her computer, pretending she hasn't heard.

How do I tell her we're up here researching an environmental thriller and it wouldn't be a good look if we were seen driving a gas guzzler. What sort of hypocrites are we, having flown 3,150 kilometres from Melbourne to get here?

'We don't know what state the roads are in,' BB Lookalike says.

'I agree. Let's take it.'

The rep hands me the keys and points us towards a Toyota Land Cruiser the colour of desert sand. I click the lock, but when I open the door and go to sit in the driver's seat, the truck is so high off the ground, I have to grab hold of the side and swing myself up.

These things should come with a mounting block.

Sitting up so high, I relish looking down at the other drivers. It's so different from my hybrid Toyota Prius, the opposite of a ute. A traffic cop in Melbourne once threatened me with a ticket when my engine cut out (as it's designed to do) in a no-stopping zone. When I tried to explain, he cut me off.

'Don't get smart with me.'

'Thank you, officer,' I said as I drove off.

Doing my bit for the planet. No need to thank me.

Not that we'll be doing much for the planet or our

budget in this tank, especially when we have to fill up at the service station. But first, we need to plan our route to Jabiru. From the map book, it looks simple enough, following the Arnhem Highway, the direct road from Darwin.

Next up is a test drive to get used to steering this monster. I wobble about the car park, reverse into a parking space, and drive off again. Once we leave the city centre and get onto the highway and the open road, we have travelled fewer than 5 kilometres before we slow down at the back of a long line of vehicles at Palmerston, a big suburban shopping strip. All the drivers up front signal and pull into the shopping centre.

'Why are they all going to the mall? Do they know something we don't?' I ask.

My partner in crime shrugs. 'Hard to tell.'

'Maybe this is the last fuel stop. It could be 250 kilometres to the next one. Let's investigate.' I follow all the other cars. As we pull in to park, I notice the trolleys piled high with beer and spirits.

I'd heard about restrictions on the sale of alcohol in the Northern Territory because of problem drinking. The hotel we're staying in is licensed, but it didn't occur to me shops in Jabiru might not sell it. We stock up with wine and beer, then grab bottled water and sandwiches from one of the lunch counters.

I click open the car. But as I put my hand on the metal handle, I snatch it away.

'Ow. It's bitten me.'

We've not even been ten minutes, but all the parking spots in the shade had been taken, and I had to park in the full sun. You could cook a pizza inside this ute. Luckily, we'd remembered to bring the car dashboard cover with us. But the steering wheel is boiling.

Bring gloves next time.

Once we've fuelled up, we hit the highway with the air conditioner on full blast. When I say highway, I mean one strip of tarmac with vehicles travelling in opposite directions, separated by nothing more than a white line in the middle.

We skip the opportunity for a photo in Humpty Doo, a town that not only has an intriguing name, but is home of the Big Boxing Crocodile (yet another one of Australia's Big Things). Ticking off all of Australia's Big Things by taking a photo of yourself with each one is a popular activity for road trippers, apparently. The Big Boxing Crocodile celebrates Australia's one and only win in the America's Cup yacht race in 1983. But the connection between yacht racing and a ginormous replica crocodile isn't clear.

As the volume of traffic on the road eases off, I glance to my left. I can't help but notice the towering rock formations scattered across the landscape. From here, they look solid.

'What do you think those are?' I ask.

'Mini volcanoes,' BB Lookalike says.

'Shall we look?' I glance up in the rear-view mirror. There's nothing behind me. I pull into a layby. This time, I put the windscreen cover over the steering wheel before getting out.

We wander over to the looming structures, batting the flies away. Up close, the strange formations are three times my height.

'Termite mounds,' BB Lookalike says.

I jump back, startled.

'Eurgh. I hope whatever built these things isn't still here.'

We take turns standing beside the termite mounds for

the obligatory photo, careful not to get too close in case a humungous insect or a snake lurks in them, ready to pounce. The ground beneath our feet is baking. We return to the ute.

We have the same problem as we did in Palmerston. The temperature has shot up to over 30C inside the cab while we were gawping at the termite mounds. I run the air-conditioner at full blast. We eat our sandwiches and slurp some water while waiting for the vehicle to cool down.

As we're about to set off, I check the rear-view mirror. A truck with its lights on full is heading straight for us. As the cab passes us, I glance to my right. It has trailers attached. The gap between the first trailer and the cab is the length of a compact car.

Then, a second trailer passes us, again with a gap. I don't know how long it's taking to pass, but it's still ongoing. And there's a third. A truck towing three huge trailers. And being about to set off behind this lorry, even in broad daylight, scares the bejesus out of me. It belongs in a Stephen King horror flick.

They have a name for them up here. A road train.

'I'd need the length of the runway at Heathrow to get past the thing,' I mutter.

'There's no hurry, we have all day,' BB Lookalike says. He's right, but as we've been taking our time, it's now 2pm and we're not even halfway, so we decide to drive straight to Jabiru. Luckily, the truck driver is on a mission and leaves me for dust.

Jabiru could best be described as a one-croc town. It was built in the 1980s, after the highway was constructed, to house Ranger mine workers and tourists visiting the national park. "Jabiru" sounds as if it ought to be an indigenous Australian word, but it's from South America.

A jabiru is a large black-necked stork, living in wetlands and billabongs. I'm hoping we see one when we go on our river tour.

We pull into the hotel's car park, unload, and walk towards the crocodile's head, which houses the reception area.

'I want to check out the eyes. They could do with eyeballs made out of glowing yellow lights, like the statue of the Madonna in that kitsch hotel in Amsterdam we stayed at back in the day.'

This hotel was built in 1987, but it must have been planned in 1986, the year the film *Crocodile Dundee* was released. While the crocodile is of spiritual significance to the traditional owners, the Gaagudju people, the film was such a big hit, it surely influenced the final design.

We eat dinner in the hotel restaurant. Crocodile is on the menu as part of the "bush tucker" selection, but I pass. I was working at Walt Disney World in Florida for the UK Disney Channel when my American colleagues insisted on ordering me an alligator starter. I played along with their macho posturing and told them I'd order black pudding on their behalf if they ever came over to England. None of them ever did. The 'gator meat was fishy, oily, chewy, and salty.

'You know who'd love this? Pluto and Goofy,' I said before diving into my glass of wine to mask the taste of the apex predator. Today, I have the local barramundi instead.

Our dining companions at the breakfast buffet the next morning are retirees on an epic journey circumnavigating Australia.

Good for them, getting out there to see this vast continent.

The Accidental Plus One

Our outing today is to look for the disused uranium mines. The first place on the map is Coronation Hill, a two-hour drive south on the Kakadu Highway, where in 1953, uranium was discovered. The main roads up here are decent and in good repair. Considering the size of the road trains plying this highway, they have to be. Today is my lucky day, as I haven't seen any yet.

At the intersection of the Kakadu Highway and Gimbat, we turn left and follow the road for the next 30km. When we arrive at Coronation Hill, I slow right down. It's eerie, deserted and littered with rusty signs, including the universal symbol for radiation, a black fan on a yellow circle.

It could be a scene from Mad Max.

As we get out of the truck, we spot another sign: "Warning: You are about to enter a Mining Lease. This area contains shafts and other mine workings. Unauthorised Entry is Prohibited." Underneath are the contact details for the Coronation Hill Project, complete with a 1950s area code and a five-digit telephone number.

'We'd better be careful where we walk,' I say. 'No one will pull us out if we fall down a mineshaft.'

There's a rustle in the grass, and a wallaby bounces off, oblivious to the dangers of radioactivity and whatever lurks underground.

Does it glow in the dark?

In the distance is a rusty-looking tin shed, no doubt the remains of some kind of living quarters for the miners. We're not game enough to walk over there in case we step somewhere we shouldn't, so we decide to stick to the main track.

Not far away, we spot some rusty old equipment and signs pointing to a display. They're attempting to explain what all this kit was used for. It all looks so primitive.

The information label reads: "The 1953 mining boom in the South Alligator River valley resulted in 13 mines being established in the region. The largest camp, El Sherana, had a population of 150 people. By 1964, an oversupply of uranium on the world market brought the price of the ore down and closed most of the mines."

How dreadful the conditions must have been for the poor wretches who worked in these mines. And they had to live out in the middle of nowhere in the searing heat.

An information label attempts a positive spin.

"The uranium industry brought development and infrastructure to the Top End. Many of the roads in this area were built to enable access to mines and processing sites... In those days, fewer environmental controls were in place or considered necessary."

It doesn't seem as if there were any environmental controls. What sort of life expectancy did those miners have? Did they even wear gloves in the way of "safety equipment?"

We stop in front of a rusty vertical tank about a metre and a half off the ground, which is described as a water heater. Where in the process it was used isn't explained. The exhibit beside it is an engine, less rusty than the water heater, which may have been used to dig the mine shafts. Alongside are some corroded billy carts or rail trolleys and a winch, which were used to carry the uranium ore from the mineshaft to the stockpile.

The last information sign describes the nearby swimming hole, now known as Gunlom Falls, where the miners went not only to relax, but to wash. It's 36C and on such a scorching hot day, I can't think of anything nicer than dipping my toes in cool water. We get back into the ute and I bump my way slowly down a rutted dirt track that passes for a road in these parts.

We'd never have done this without a 4WD.

When we arrive at the falls, it's packed full of holiday-makers with huge vehicles and camping equipment. We squeeze into the last parking space. I kick myself for not bringing my swimming costume. BB Lookalike brought his and joins the line of blokes all walking into the water next to each other. A sign reads, "Watch out for crocodiles."

'What sort of crocodiles?' I ask one of the men heading eagerly towards the falls.

'Freshies. They won't harm yer. You'll be alright.' Freshies, or fresh water crocodiles, are smaller and less-aggressive than their lethal saltwater cousins. There's strength in numbers and all the guys come out of the water with their fingers and toes intact.

The next day, we take the day off from our book research and go to view rock art at Ubirr. We have the place to ourselves. Then, we join a river cruise to look at bird life and saltwater crocodiles. The cruise passengers are all foreign visitors.

All the Aussies are camping at Gunlom Falls.

On the way back to Jabiru, we spot another road train ahead. Life is short enough without dicing with death on the highway trying to overtake a monster truck.

The following day, we set off for the highlight of this trip—the chance to undertake some primary research for our novel. And it's not every day we get to go on a tour of a uranium mine.

The Ranger mine, owned by a subsidiary of the British-Australian multi-national company Rio Tinto, hosts slick PR tours. We arrive at the mine and are given a safety briefing before being issued hi-vis tabards and white hard hats. There are seven of us on the tour, including a mum and dad with their two kids, a boy and a girl about twelve and fourteen.

The girl squirms. 'Aww, Mum, do we have to?'

'Shh, they'll hear. I told you it's educational.' The daughter rolls her eyes. The son looks at his shoes, as our tour guide is busy inspecting our footwear. We all heeded the memo and wore enclosed shoes. BB Lookalike and I have gone one step further and have put on walking boots. My feet are boiling in this heat.

We scramble aboard the luxury minibus with air-conditioning on at full blast. Once we're loaded, there's a glitzy video presentation about the mine as we head off.

As we drive the perimeter of this vast complex, I stare, transfixed. Stretching out in front of and below us, as far as we can see, are three open-cast mines. Inside the mines are what look from this distance like tiny yellow toddler toys: bulldozers, excavators, front-loaders and trucks, all going about their business. This is the second-largest uranium mine in the world, we are told. The ore is exported offshore to Asia, Europe and the USA. So far, there is no domestic market as Australia has strict federal laws banning nuclear power. The one nuclear plant in Sydney produces radioisotopes for hospitals.

'Here's why you need those covered shoes,' the guide says as the minibus pulls up. 'Okay, folks, we're about to walk on some low-level radioactive rocks. Mind your step and keep together as a group.'

I've hiked over a few volcanic rocks in New Zealand. The sensation feels similar.

'Righto, we're going to take you back down to the plant where you can observe the processing operation. Do you have questions?' We have a million questions we keep to ourselves as we pose as tourists, one of which is who will pay for the clean-up once the mine is no longer productive.

The Accidental Plus One

I'm too busy taking photos to have time to make notes as we get up close to the maze of pipework, snaking its way around the refinery.

That evening, I go through my photos. They will be our inspiration for our prototype refinery, which turns out to be an oil one, rather than uranium, as this best serves our story. The last scene, though, is set in Kakadu National Park, where a key character observed that, "the scar of the Jabiru mine appeared raw, a wound in the green skin of the country."

On our last morning in the Northern Territory, I pull out onto the northbound highway for a leisurely drive back to Darwin. Right in front of us is a road train. I slow down and pull out to look in front of the vehicle, but the tarmac is baking hot and the road ahead shimmers into a mirage in the distance.

Then, there's a clear line of sight. It's now or never. I signal, pull out, and put my foot down.

I hope the kangaroos are tucked up under a tree somewhere and not planning to bounce across my path.

At the point of no return, when I'm level with the truck, I keep my eyes fixed on the road ahead. I press the accelerator for all it's worth and fly along the road, and at last I'm clear of this juggernaut.

But as I pull back to the left, I spot the vehicle in front —a nondescript-looking blue truck. On the back is a warning sign, stating the contents are corrosive, and in case of an accident, the advice is to dial the police or fire brigade on 000. Underneath the sign is the now familiar black fan on a yellow background with the word "radioactive."

As I overtake, I glance at the cab.

'It's one driver on a lonely road. How come their security's so lax? What if he was ambushed and his cargo stolen?' And with this scenario, we bat our ideas back and forth for a possible sub-plot for the first Stephen Connor mystery, *Revolution Earth* (see the Also by section at the end of this book).

Postscript

In 2021 Ranger Uranium Mine closed. Rio Tinto has taken over the rehabilitation of the site amid spiralling costs. The clean-up operation is expected to exceed $AUD 2.2 billion and it is projected to be completed by 2029 at the earliest.

15

Right Turn From Left

One evening, I sit down to watch the true-crime series *Underbelly*, set in gangland Melbourne, as I'm wondering if there's a way to tie this story into the plot of our thriller. A detective in the fictional programme bears a startling resemblance to the previous owner of our house. Was it intentional or a coincidence? You don't have to be all that clever to work out who they are.

No wonder the family has to keep moving house.

That night, my sleep is plagued with bad dreams. After a particularly scary one, I'm woken by headlights on full beam as a car drives slowly down the service road, towards the back entrance to our house and garage. I check my watch. It's 3am.

My heart races and I go into flight mode. I run down the stairs, checking all the locks—front door, windows, patio doors and the internal access to the garage. I look out over the inky blackness of the back garden. The only way in is over the 2-metre fence.

There could be a rational explanation. They're lost, and they can't find the way out. But at 3am—in the middle of suburbia?

All I can think about is the connection between the cops who used to live here and the TV series.

What if the killer doesn't know they've moved house?

I go back upstairs and peer out through the window. There's no sign of the car. I'm wide awake and go downstairs again to make myself a pot of tea. The dog lifts her head, yawns and goes back to sleep.

Thanks to my overactive imagination, the day turns into a very long one.

Sitting in the house alone writing about violent crime isn't healthy. I need to engage with real people as opposed to fictional ones. And once the renovations are done, I'm going back to work as a consultant for the relocation company which found us our rented place. I need to get more familiar with the area.

Navigating my way across Auckland was a breeze, as the city has so many distinctive landmarks. I could tell where I was by looking at either the Sky Tower in the CBD, New Zealand's tallest building, or Rangitoto Island, the distinct volcano in the middle of the Waitemata Harbour. Even when I was working on the North Shore, on the northern side of the Auckland Harbour Bridge, Rangitoto was still visible.

However, I came unstuck when I went to an unfamiliar part of Greater Auckland with a client who wanted to live in the country and commute to the city centre. At the northernmost navigable point at the top of the Waitemata Harbour is Riverhead, a country town. The properties out there are 10-acre blocks tucked down long country roads. By the time I got to the last one, I was so lost, I'd forgotten how to get back to Riverhead. There were no landmarks I recognised and if I wasn't careful, we'd be driving in circles for the rest of the afternoon. Luckily, the client didn't notice as she was so absorbed in her search for the perfect property.

Once I spotted water, I could work out where I was. I kept the water on my left, which led me down to the main road. And there, in the distance, were Rangitoto and the Sky Tower.

Trying to find my way in Melbourne is a much tougher proposition. Imagine the entire population of New Zealand living in a city with an urban sprawl the size of Greater Los Angeles. And most of my clients want to live in the sought-after eastern suburbs, which are flat with no distinct landmarks. I can't even tell you when Albert Park becomes Middle Park or when South Yarra becomes Toorak because I live in the unfashionable part of town, across the sprawling Westgate Bridge, then 6 kilometres west on a peninsula. My Toyota Prius isn't new enough to have an inbuilt GPS. I could get a Garmin or something similar, but I decide against it as I need to see where I'm going. And besides, how am I going to learn to navigate if I'm relying on technology?

There are other challenges we didn't have in New Zealand—hook turns and trams. For the first couple of jobs picking up in the city, I pretend hook turns don't exist by planning my route, turning left in the centre and avoiding turning right across the tram tracks. But I can't avoid them forever and have to get to grips with them.

I get up early one Sunday morning and drive into the centre of the city. A hook turn is a manoeuvre at an intersection and there are 50 intersections in Melbourne where they apply. There will be a warning sign: Right Turn from Left Only. As you drive towards the intersection, get in the left lane, indicating right. When the light turns green, drive into the intersection, but pull left, away from any pedestrian crossings. As soon as the light turns green into the street you want to turn into, you can complete the turn.

It's simple and stress-free if yours is the first car, but what if it's the third and the light changes at the point of no return? You risk being mown down by a wall of traffic, including a tram with lights on and bells ringing. And you can't chicken out about the turn and stay in the box as you'll block the intersection.

After an accident when a turning bus in Manchester side-swiped my car on the driver's side, I'm nervous about being alongside tanks and other super-sized vehicles, of which there are many in Melbourne. I still shudder when I find myself next to a tram. The newer trams have three carriages and when they turn a corner, they take up the entire intersection.

But once I master the hook turn, I get cocky. I approach a stop as an older-style tram rumbles past. A hand giving a royal wave pops up on the left above the door. I put my foot down to go past it, and the next minute, there's a ding, ding, ding as the doors fling open and passengers pile out. I come to a screeching stop and am stuck beside the tram. We are right outside the Royal Melbourne Hospital, and a woman on crutches hops down from the tram and waves a crutch at my face. I slink down in my seat and avert my eyes.

Next time I see a tram giving a royal wave, I'll remember it means stop.

16

The Price of Gold

'This is Docklands,' I say as I drive my client Rohan, a computer engineer from India, past empty apartment blocks interspersed with corporate headquarters. 'You'd be better off in the CBD than here as there's a distinct lack of shops. Don't worry, I'll find you somewhere within walking distance.'

This is the first time he's travelled overseas, he confides.

'I'm excited but also a little apprehensive,' he says.

'It'll differ from back home, especially the culture and the lifestyle. Do you need a SIM, or a public transport card?'

'Thank you, I have the SIM and I won't need to go on public transport as you're going to find me an apartment walking distance to the office.'

I'm going to try my best.

This should be a straightforward relocation, but apart from being close enough for him to walk to the bank where he works, he's not given me a brief of what sort of property he's looking for. I change tack.

'As it's such a lovely day, and the visibility is good, how

about we go up our tallest building, so I can show you the layout of the city?' I have two free tickets for the Eureka Tower Skydeck which are about to expire and this seems a good way to use them. I find a parking spot for an hour nearby. As we ride the lift to the 88th floor, Rohan shakes his head from side to side.

'My ears are popping,' he says.

'Mine too.'

When we arrive at the top, the view stretches from the Dandenongs right down to the Mornington Peninsula.

Better do my tourist spiel.

'Over to the east, there are the Dandenong Ranges, home to some of Australia's largest trees, the mountain ash.'

Rohan shrugs.

Why am I talking about trees?

'Let's walk this way,' I say, steering him back in the opposite direction. 'Over to the west in the background is Williamstown, where there's a beach, and in the foreground Docklands, where the office is.'

And which has no redeeming features.

Rohan nods. I face south, towards Albert Park Lake, known by car enthusiasts the world over.

'Are you interested in motor racing?'

Rohan turns to me, his face lighting up.

'See down there?' He nods again. 'It's the home of the Melbourne Grand Prix.'

'Can we visit it after this? And can you take my picture to send to my friends and family?'

'Of course we can. Seen enough up here?'

'Let's go.'

We get to Albert Park in fewer than ten minutes and there are loads of places to park along the track, which is open to both cars and bicycles. It's early afternoon and before rush hour, so in between the bikes and the cars, I'm able to take the photo Rohan asked for. As we drive back towards town, he's less fidgety.

'We have a half day left in our schedule, so if there's anything else you want to do, we have time.'

'Actually, there is something.'

Then I remembered that in an email he'd told me he was a cricket fan.

Please don't ask me to take you to the Melbourne Cricket Ground. The only thing I know about cricket is Shane Warne.

'Could you take me to see a kangaroo?'

I wasn't expecting that.

'If I came to India, I'd be asking to see a tiger.'

'I have never seen a tiger either.'

'You are the first client who has asked for a kangaroo, but I think I can find you one.'

A visitor from Sweden was disappointed when they didn't see any kangaroos in Albert Park. And although it is a little far-fetched to think you'd see one in the city centre, once you get out into the suburbs, there's a wildlife corridor stretching along Plenty Gorge Park in South Morang and a smaller habitat on the La Trobe University campus at Bundoora.

I once dropped BB Lookalike off at La Trobe for a meeting early one morning. We set off at 7am from Williamstown, 30km away. It was already rush hour, and he had to be there for 8.30am. We reached the campus at 8.15, and the sun was still low in the sky as it was winter. As I turned into the university grounds, I did a double take. A herd of grazing Eastern Greys lifted their heads at the sound of the car. There were females with their offspring and a big male who seemed very much in charge. They soon worked out we weren't a threat and carried on grazing.

As the best chances of seeing wild kangaroos are at dawn and dusk, going up there isn't an option at this time of the day. The zoo it will have to be.

'Let's see how much time we have left after we've found you somewhere to live,' I say, handing Rohan the list of properties we are about to see. They're all in the city centre and within walking distance to both the Docklands office and the bank's other main building on Collins Street.

Within his budget of $400 a week, we find an apartment with a separate bedroom, which is a big plus, as many of the others in his price range are studios. It has a modern kitchen down one wall with an induction hob and an oven. Rohan scratches his head when inspecting the hob.

'How do you use these? We don't have them back at home.'

'You cook?' I ask, sounding surprised.

'Yes, but on the stovetop.'

'An induction hob heats quicker compared with a regular electric one. Modern pots and pans work on it. I'd show you, but the electricity isn't switched on.'

'Okay, I'll get used to it,' Rohan says. 'I wish to take this place. Is it okay if one of my colleagues shares with me?'

The agent nods her head in agreement. 'It should be fine.'

'Shall we sign you up?' I say, relieved we've found somewhere this fast. Once he's signed the lease, we head off to Victoria Market, a huge fresh food market right in the city, which is a couple of blocks away. I cut through to the fruit and vegetable section.

'What do you cook?'

'I'm vegetarian and I cook curries.' He casts his eyes over the selection. There are plenty of different vegetables, but these are better suited to Western dishes, although there are basics which feature in pretty much every cuisine.

'Which region of India are you from?' I ask.

'Gujarat,' he says.

'What vegetables feature in a Gujarati curry?'

'Bhindi, bitter gourd, brinjal, potato, spinach. And we serve those with dahl, chapatti, or rice.' Brinjal I know is aubergine, or eggplant as it's called here. But I don't think he means the large eggplants used in European cooking, but the smaller ones, which I know as Thai eggplants. Bhindi is okra or lady's fingers. I scan the fresh produce stalls until I spot one specialising in Asian vegetables.

'Let's go over to this one,' I say. The display looks promising, although the produce is more suited to wok style cooking. Bok choy, Chinese cabbage and Thai basil won't be much good to him, but at least they have the right eggplants and large bunches of coriander.

'Anything you can't find here, you should get in your nearest Indian supermarket, which is close by. We can go after this.'

'Let's take a look here first,' Rohan says. He wanders about, checking out all the stalls.

'Find what you wanted?'

'Some things.'

I look at my watch. 'We can either go to check out this Indian grocery store together, or I have enough time to take you to see a kangaroo.'

'I can go to a grocery store any time. Let's see a kangaroo and maybe a koala bear.'

'I'll even throw in a platypus and a Tasmanian Devil.'

It'll be my luck, none of them will be on show now I've promised. Too bad I don't heed my advice: don't promise what you can't deliver.

I'm always doing this. One of the first of the IT crowd

from Bangalore I'd helped move, I told to ask me anything. I was expecting the usual: customs, habits, things Australian. We were driving along Collins Street, Melbourne's most opulent shopping street, and I was busy explaining the gold rush financed the ornate nineteenth century buildings when my client's ears pricked up.

He turned to me. 'What is the price of gold?'

You've brought this one upon yourself. He's taken you at your word.

I struggled to get the words out.

'When I said...' I began.

Forget it. Now let's see how you get yourself out of this.

'I don't have the figure in my head. But we could look it up together once we've reached our destination.'

'I can do it myself,' he said, sounding disappointed. I relayed this story to a friend who came up with the answer —it isn't worth buying gold in Australia as he'd have to pay 10% GST (Goods and Services Tax).

Why didn't I think of that at the time?

As we are looking at the animals in Melbourne Zoo, Rohan tells me in his home state, there are lions. I have heard about Asiatic lions, but had forgotten they come from India.

Of course they do. You've read The Jungle Book.

Luckily, we tick off all the animals I've promised. So at least I'm able to say I've delivered the right apartment, a photo opportunity at the Grand Prix track and an insight into Australia's unique wildlife.

17

The Beer Taster

On evenings and weekends, we repaint the dining and sitting rooms. The first to go is the brown feature wall, which takes three coats of primer to remove the old colour before we can repaint in cool-climate Scandinavian shades. But the work is stop-start while we wait for our new kitchen to be completed, with me project managing all the different trades.

As soon as the paint is dry and the shiny new kitchen installed, water pours through the ceiling from the upstairs balcony next to our bedroom down into the sitting room, behind the front door.

What is it with houses Down Under?

This one, though, is modern—ten years old, and it was architect-designed. Which means nothing when you try to claim against the building guarantee. Our claim is rejected, as the guarantee expired a month earlier. It costs us $10,000 to fix the leak, which we never budgeted for. So much for choosing a new house, thinking we wouldn't need to spend any money on maintenance.

No wonder the vendors gave us a good deal.

We decide to have our nondescript suburban back garden landscaped. I can't believe how much work it entails and how expensive it is, so I say yes to every relocation job I'm offered. But it will make our house stand out amongst all the other townhouses in the development, should we ever need to sell. Wendy, a friend I make in Williamstown, has the most glorious garden, fittingly as she is a garden designer. She lives in a beautiful wooden villa and her property oozes character. It reminds me so much of our place in Kohimarama.

Meanwhile, in the day job, I continue to help other people who have upped sticks to find a home in Melbourne. Noah and his young family have relocated from Denmark so he can continue his rabbinical studies in Kew. Until this opportunity came up, he'd spent the past four years working full-time and studying at night. The family jumped at the chance to move to Australia, despite having no relatives here to give them advice and help. And their young children don't know any English—only Danish and Hebrew. But Noah is single-minded about making their move a success. He is excited about his future career, and his enthusiasm is infectious.

'It was so different in Denmark,' he confides.

'In what way?'

'It's a major career change. I only found my calling a few years back, and you'll never guess what I used to do for a living.'

He has a delightful sense of humour, always laughing at some absurdity, so I feel comfortable enough in his presence to venture.

'I don't know. Stand-up comedian?'

'Close. How about a beer taster for Carlsberg.'

'You're pulling my leg,' I say, suppressing a giggle.

'I knew you'd like it,' Noah says, wearing a mischievous grin. He's right. I love it.

Before I met Noah and Hannah, I knew very little about the food rules associated with being Orthodox. At a TV company I worked for in Manchester, a Jewish colleague used to bring along a kosher meal if we were going out to eat out after work. He would ask the restaurant to reheat it for him, so he could join in. So, I wanted to know how Noah navigated this requirement with his unique job.

'How did it work, tasting beer and keeping kosher?'

'I could taste it, but I couldn't swallow it,' he says, laughing. If it's similar to tea tasting, which I observed when filming for a documentary, it's exacting work. At Twinings in London, the tasters sip a tablespoon of brewed tea out of tiny cups. After every taste, they must spit it out before refreshing their palates and trying again. But a beer taster must have to exercise restraint not to swallow, otherwise they'd be drunk at work.

I ask Noah what happens when he travels abroad and gets quizzed at immigration about his unique profession. Quick as a flash, he comes back with 'an offer to swap jobs.'

At least some border officials have a sense of humour.

Much as I enjoy working with Noah and his family, finding them a home is a bigger challenge than I thought. Kew is an expensive area, and Noah's modest salary will only stretch to an apartment. Hannah is keen to work to supplement their income, but looking after their two young children is a full-time job. And she has pastoral commitments within the community to fulfil as a rabbi's wife.

But the biggest challenge is their home has to be within easy walking distance of the synagogue. Members of the

Orthodox Jewish community may not move beyond the confines of the distance they can walk on Shabbat (Jewish Sabbath). I first get out a map of Kew, pinpoint the synagogue, and work out a rough 5-kilometre radius. But as they have young children who need to ride in a buggy, I narrow it down to 2 kilometres. Even this distance is a stretch, but at least if they are all going to the synagogue, Noah can take his turn wheeling the pushchair rather than Hannah all the time.

Noah and Hannah are prepared to look at anything, no matter its condition.

'I might not be able to get you an apartment with a balcony.'

'We can do without if it's in the right location. Our place in Copenhagen had no outside space, so the children won't miss it,' Hannah says.

'It encourages us to take the children on walks,' Hannah adds.

I find an older-style apartment on the first floor of a converted house. The stairs are narrow, and I'm worried they'd struggle to get the buggy up and down. As the agent is with us, I ask her if it would be possible to ask the landlord if they could leave the buggy in the communal hallway.

'I see what you mean. I'll check,' she says.

The conversion into two apartments took place at least 20 years ago, before building regulations stipulated a minimum width for a staircase. The couple will need help to move furniture in and out.

We walk into the hallway of the apartment, and Hannah and Noah's faces light up. The door to the living room is ajar. It's a sunny summer day outside, but leafy plane trees filter the light. This is the apartment's best feature.

'We're part of the natural world up here,' Noah says.

'This is where we'd be spending most of our time, and it's lovely,' Hannah says.

'Shall we check out the kitchen?'

I've read up about the requirements for a kosher kitchen, which must be a space large enough to split into two separate areas for the storage, preparation, utensils, pots, and pans for milk and meat. To my eyes, the square kitchen, with the double sink facing the window, surrounded by three walls of storage and bench tops, is too small. But Hannah has fallen in love with the apartment and is finding hacks to solve the problem.

'It's bigger than the Copenhagen place.'

This is a first. Never has a client compared their previous home unfavourably with what I can show them. Often, everything about the life they left behind was bigger and better.

'How will it work with the two fridges?' I ask.

'Easy. We can put the milk one in the space here,' Hannah says, pointing to the gap where the fridge/freezer goes, 'and we can keep the small fridge for meat in the hallway.' With this attitude, these two can make anything work.

The kitchen sorted, we turn our attention to the bedrooms and the bathroom. The bedrooms are compact, but at least they come with built-in wardrobes.

'We love it. It's perfect,' Hannah says.

I turn to the agent. 'Can we put in an application?'

She nods enthusiastically.

'Of course.'

Their application, pending reference checks, is approved, and as I drop them back to their serviced apartment, they are walking on air. Noah grabs my hand and pumps it. Hannah grabs the other one. These two are adorable.

I am invited to Noah's official ordination ceremony, which will be at the synagogue, followed by a celebratory meal. This will be my first visit to a synagogue, and I don't know what to expect.

Back in the day, Mum wore a black mantilla when she took me to Mass in Kuala Lumpur. In England, she wore a headscarf similar to the Queen. In New Zealand, she never bothered, even though officially, it took until 1983 to end the requirement for Catholic women to cover their heads in church. And so, the first thing I do is check up on the dress code, and to my relief, I don't need to cover my hair. The key condition is to cover any flesh from the neck down.

In the synagogue in Kew, the men and women are segregated, with the men downstairs and the women upstairs. As I arrive, Hannah welcomes me, takes me upstairs and introduces me to the women there. From my balcony seating area, I can see everywhere. Excited children tear up and down the stairs. What a contrast with my religious boarding school where seven-year-olds were ordered to keep quiet, especially once the priest entered the church. We children pretended to follow the Latin Mass even though we didn't understand a word, knelt when we were told and did as the priest instructed until the end of the boring hour-long service.

This service goes on for two hours. No wonder the women are chatting away, talking about their kids, complaining about the price of food, gossiping and not paying much attention to what's happening below. Except when the time comes to bless the Torah. Then, everyone goes quiet and bows their heads. It reminds me of the liturgy of the Eucharist in Mass when I couldn't resist watching the priest, although I should have been praying.

After synagogue, I attend the formal lunch celebrations, where we toast and celebrate Noah's ordination. How generous of them to invite me.

If we humans could only focus on the similarities rather than the differences between the various religions, the world would be a much safer place.

18

Will We Still Call Australia Home?

After four years of working on our house, we've transformed it. I'm still not sold on living on this purpose-built estate as we need a car to get to places, but the coastal walks and the wildlife are a bonus.

With my clients, I continue to sing Melbourne's praises, even if I don't always have the feels. At least I have choices, unlike my next clients, Rebecca and Jon, who I take on an orientation visit. For this South African family, not only is their homeland no longer safe, but their low-value rands mean their budget won't stretch beyond the outer suburbs of Melbourne. They want to be near the water, so I take them to Patterson Lakes, where the properties they can afford are identical three-bedroom townhouses.

Rebecca bursts into tears when she sees the first house. She must be used to a higher standard of living.

'It'll be a stopgap. Once I earn in Australian dollars, we'll be able to afford a better place,' Jon says, trying but failing to comfort his wife while I beat a retreat. According to rumours, Rebecca has found Melbourne challenging and explored Perth as an alternative. She may not realise

Western Australia, in the grip of a resources boom, can be more expensive for renters than Melbourne.

Rebecca and Jon are not the first people I have assisted who don't want to move to Melbourne. Another family I worked with resented coming here because they thought it might disrupt their teenage children's education. "Reluctant movers," ambivalent about the destination country and moving for a promotion and a bigger salary, are often the most demanding clients to please. When I'm sent a long wish list, my job can take twice as long, as I spend my time managing expectations.

As I think about our long-term future and where we want to end up, I feed off this negativity. I ask BB Lookalike what he thinks and if he wants to grow old in Australia. He tells me no. And I'm relieved. It's New Zealand or the UK for me now. I'm leaning towards the UK as most of our family lives there. I don't want to remain so far away from them forever; otherwise, we're in danger of becoming estranged.

Christmas time is hard away from family and I feel very isolated out here in suburbia. My neighbours have family visiting over the festive season while we take ourselves off on road trips. One year, we drove to Sydney to visit friends, taking the coastal route via Eden. Another time, we spent Christmas up in the high country of New South Wales with Zebedee.

The event that really made me question why we lived in this unforgiving land took place in early 2009. For three days, the temperature in Melbourne hit 43 degrees Celsius. As I was showing a client a property in Brighton, by 10am, it was 35 degrees, the road was a shimmering mirage, and I was desperate to find a parking space in the shade. Because we were in a leafy area, my strategy worked most of the time. One house we viewed had a glorious-looking swimming pool in the back garden. My client and I glanced at each other. The water was calling; we'd have done anything to jump in.

A week after the blazing temperatures, strong winds with gusts up to 100kph whipped up across the state. The ground was tinder-dry because we'd had no rain for weeks. On Saturday 7 February, temperatures in Melbourne hit 46C. In the countryside, the strong winds ripped down a main power cable in Kilmore East. The sparks caused a catastrophic bushfire on top of the fires already burning in Gippsland and other parts of Victoria. Known as Black Saturday, this event filled news broadcasts with horror stories of residents who left it too late to evacuate and couldn't outrun the firestorm. The newspapers wrote about the 173 people who were killed and the 7,500 survivors who lost their homes.

As well as the human victims, the bushfire had a devastating impact on the farm animals and wildlife in the area. One photograph I'll never forget is the image of a firefighter giving a burnt koala water out of a bottle. Against the odds, Sam, the koala, survived the deadly fires and became a symbol of hope for all the human survivors.

Smoke from the countryside drifted over Melbourne, and the pollution hung in the air for weeks. By 9 February, the bushfire smoke had travelled over 3,000km across the Tasman Sea, reaching New Zealand.

My escape from the sorrow of the deadly fires couldn't come soon enough. BB Lookalike and I returned to the UK for a few weeks during the mid-year university break to catch up with family and friends. During this trip, I spilt the beans that if the right job turned up in the south of

England, we'd consider moving back. We wanted to live within an hour's train commute from London. I drew a radius from Winchester in the southwest right up to the Chilterns.

We viewed an 18th-century house with a picture-postcard walled garden in Farnham. Heritage-listed, it had some challenging low ceilings, especially in the tiny third bedroom. Another one we saw was in Berkshire, in the heart of the village of Bray. Bray is home to two Michelin-starred restaurants, one of which is the famous Fat Duck, owned by global superstar chef Heston Blumenthal. The Fat Duck has three Michelin stars, and it's not only where you go to eat dinner. The PR literature pitches it as a "sensorium"—where the brain receives and processes stimuli. And there was me thinking it was my stomach I'd be feeding. When you add the cost of the compulsory tasting menu to matching wines, it's £300 a head, or £100 per hour per person.

Luckily, the rock-star chef owns a more affordable venue nearby, the Hind's Head, a 15th century pub. We decided to have lunch there before our viewing. We sat next to the cosy fire, which was lit even though it was meant to be summer. I had a prawn cocktail, a 70s classic. There was no sign of the limp lettuce and soggy prawn concoction of yesteryear here. This one had a bed of crispy lettuce on top of which sat fat, juicy prawns married with a perfectly flavoured sauce balancing salt, umami, acid and heat. BB Lookalike had a warm Scotch egg, with the yolk runny in the middle. With our drinks, we paid less than £20 a head.

'Imagine if this was our local,' I said.

'Don't get too excited; let's see the house first.' From the photographs, it appeared to be neglected and in need of work. I didn't know why I couldn't pinpoint the location on Google Maps. It was either done for privacy or to hide something.

In the case of this house, it was the latter.

'Look, it's near the Fat Duck,' I said. 'I wonder if we'll have trouble with fat-duck-mobiles parking in front of our house.' There were double yellow lines along the side of the road, but that wouldn't stop the super-rich. Rules are for losers. They'd park there and pay the fine.

'It's not near the Fat Duck, it's right next door,' BB Lookalike said.

'Putting the braying into Bray. We'll hear all the comings and the goings. Rich drunks, late at night, tottering about on their Jimmy Choos.'

'We're here now. We may as well look at it.'

It's funny how the only day the agent could show us is a Monday when the restaurant is shut.

I checked my notes. I saw why I—and Google Maps—was confused. We were viewing the first house on Church Lane, and the Fat Duck was the first building on High Street.

It was a three-bedroom terrace, and the front door opened straight onto the street.

Not a good start.

The rooms were small and it needed some serious money spent on it. Out the back was the potential to create a patio garden. But from my vantage point, looking through the window from the poky third bedroom to the restaurant right next door, I spotted three huge containers with lids. The Fat Duck's bins. We'd be getting sensory overload, but unlike Heston's customers, we'd be inhaling smelly food waste. And if you've ever stayed in a hotel with a room at the back next to the restaurant, you'll know noisy vehicles collect the waste at dawn.

Even though the house wasn't for us, we had earned bragging rights—we ate at one of Heston's restaurants.

A year after the bushfires and almost five years to the day that we sold our dream home in Kohimarama, we put the Williamstown house on the market. We'll rent while we wait for job opportunities to come up in the UK. BB Lookalike will only move if certain conditions are met. And it's not going to be easy. Fair enough—he's not the one with the burning desire to decamp.

19

The Kangaroo Route

With the addition of native Australian plants and a statement rock the colour of the outback outside the front door for instant kerb appeal, the house and garden are ready. We choose the agent who showed me the house on Douglas Parade in Newport to handle the sale and reinstate the same tried and tested routine for the Open for Inspections.

Lights on.

All signs of a dog living at the house removed, including scouring the upstairs bath for black Labrador hair.

A bowl of lemons on the stone island benchtop.

Hot Club de France on the sound system.

As the agent approaches, BB Lookalike, the dog, and I pile into the car.

This is a complete leap of faith. What if we don't sell? Then what do we do?

BB Lookalike will only move to an art school in the south of England, and the job must be a research professorship.

The Accidental Plus One

What are the odds of a job like this turning up? 100:1?

We sell the house in three weeks to a buyer who has fallen in love with the outdoor space Wendy designed for us. Wendy is delighted the garden she created is thriving as her health deteriorates after a devastating diagnosis of Stage 4 ovarian cancer. In between getting ready for our move, I visit her first in hospitals in Melbourne, where she has to have emergency surgery, then the Peter Mac Cancer Centre, where she is receiving chemotherapy. I help her out with her garden straight after chemo when she is at her weakest. She shrugs off her illness when I'm with her, determined to make the most of our remaining time together.

With all this going on, BB Lookalike and I are pressed to find somewhere else to live now we've sold the house. I ask the agent if she can find us a place to rent for six months, with the option to renew if we need to. She comes back to me straight away.

'You'll never guess,' she says. 'The house you saw in Newport is up for rent.'

'What are the chances? We don't even need to look at it again. I still have the photographs and the floorplan.'

'That's a yes, then,' she says, laughing.

'I get to live in the house I wanted to buy, after all.'

Everything is falling into place with the townhouse sold and an impending move to Newport. I can't believe BB Lookalike is willing to move again to make me happy. He is a saint. But he's also made it clear he won't move for any job. And if he doesn't find that perfect job, we could be renting for some time.

One evening, while ploughing through emails, BB Lookalike gets a message out of the blue from an old friend sounding him out about a job at the art school in Winchester.

'Art school? Winchester? I didn't even know it had an art school...'

'Part of the University of Southampton. Russell Group. Worth moving for.'

'Southampton in Hampshire? The Home Counties?' I stand there, open-mouthed.

'It's for a Research Professor. No actual teaching involved...'

Only every single box ticked on his list!

I haven't been to Winchester, but I've visited Hampshire many times and the countryside is gorgeous. The South Downs National Park, one of my favourite places in England, covers part of the county and extends to the next one, West Sussex, where my father grew up and we owned a house. I played up on the chalk downland at Highdown with my brother and sister, behind the village of Ferring, in the National Park. I pretended I was riding a winged horse until the pester power worked on my parents and I was allowed to have lessons on a real one.

BB Lookalike is shortlisted, and the online job interviews take place on a warm evening in late autumn. I catch a glimpse of his outfit as he prepares to be grilled via Skype. He has on a bright shirt, but as he's only going to be visible from above the waist, he has opted for shorts instead of trousers.

I hope he doesn't have to get up and walk out of the room in the middle of it...

He flies through the interview, is offered and accepts the job, and we plan to move back to the UK, ready for a start date in March 2011. My first phone call is to the vet, as Zebedee is now thirteen, which is old for a Labrador. She has poor eyesight and spinal stenosis, which is treated with Metacam pain-relief medication.

'If you are going to take her back to the UK, she needs to go as soon as possible,' the vet advises. 'I'll give her Metacam before she travels, but she'll need to be checked out at the other end.' The problem is we won't be ready to leave for another six months, so I'll have to find a temporary home for her in England in the interim. I call my sister, who agrees to take her.

Thank goodness. What would we do without family?

The pet relocation company I used to fly Zebedee from New Zealand finds us a flight leaving in three weeks. Exporting a dog to the UK from Australia is simple compared with importing one. And yet again, we have avoided quarantine. But she is nothing like the young, healthy, vibrant dog who moved with us Down Under ten years ago. I'm putting a senior dog on another gruelling long-haul journey.

I stay up all night tracking her flight via Singapore. It lands at the stopover at the coolest time of the day, before dawn local time, and she is checked over and given water. But it's the next leg, the 13 hours non-stop from Singapore to Heathrow, I worry about. I watch the little dot of her aircraft on a flight tracking website as it takes off, heading north. By the time it's over India four hours later, I can't stay awake any longer and am in danger of falling asleep in front of my laptop.

Fly well, Zebedee.

Later that day, I wake up to see the flashing blip in the sky about to cross the English Channel. When she arrives, the Heathrow Animal Reception Centre will admit her and administer pain relief for her spinal stenosis. A family member is driving all the way from the West Country to pick her up and take her to her home away from home for the next six months.

Zebedee takes a few days to recover, my sister informs me, but bounces back and has a remarkable second lease of life. Her favourite spot in the garden overlooks a construction yard. At lunchtime, when it's fine, the workers eat outdoors. She's an old dog with poor eyesight, but has yet to lose her sense of smell. Labradors are food monsters, so when the coast is clear and nobody is watching, she slides down the bank and straight into the builders' yard one lunchtime. Many sandwiches later, she is spotted and taken home, after which my sister puts up a fence. Zebedee spends the next few months in the maximum security garden, staring at the wall.

Back in Newport, BB Lookalike and I are dogless for the first time in thirteen years. As soon as I wake up, I go downstairs on auto-pilot and head towards the back door to let Zebedee out. But there is no pad, pad, pad of dog paws on the wooden floor. When he works from home, BB Lookalike schedules his day to fit in the morning or the afternoon walk. We keep up the afternoon ritual and walk together as it's too lonely to go solo.

Although our house feels silent, next door isn't. We like our neighbours, but Trudy holds conversations on her phone at full volume in the back garden. I try to blot out what she is saying, but when Trudy shouts, 'Oi, Pansy, stop eating the strawberries,' I do a double-take.

Isn't fruit good for kids?

A Pitbull terrier, accessorised with a pink collar, bounds across to Trudy.

Ahh, Pansy must be the dog.

We enjoy living in the house in Newport, but as autumn turns to winter, we find the downsides. The staircase requires care, as it's a lethal combination of a challenging width, no handrail and a narrow depth to each step. We have to walk down sideways, like a skier coming down a slippery mountain. And the house is cold in winter because of the high ceilings, the single-glazed windows and no insulation. But because it's semi-detached, we benefit from the heat from next door.

In the depths of winter, it rains. In the upstairs hallway, I step into a puddle of water. I look up to see the steady drip, drip, drip descending from above me.

Not another leaky house!

But this roof isn't our problem for once, as it's the landlord's job to fix it. He sends a plumber, while we'd send a roofer in the UK. The plumber/roofer patches up the hole, and the repair lasts for a bit before we have to get the bucket out again to catch the drips.

If we'd bought this house, we'd be paying to fix it. Given its age, it will need a new roof.

We time our departure from Australia in the middle of February, at the height of the southern summer. We plan to fly via New Zealand to say goodbye to friends, then spend a few days of rest and relaxation in the South Pacific, in the Cook Islands. When we arrive back in England, it will be the last day of winter and spring will follow—or so we hope.

We can't find any serviced accommodation in Winchester, let alone anything dog-friendly. The best our movers can come up with is in Southampton, 20 minutes away by train. I find a short-term holiday let, a one-bedroom flat almost opposite the Winchester Art School. From the photos, it looks small. I'm hoping we can find somewhere to rent longer-term as soon as possible.

The movers arrive with a 20-foot container to pack up our stuff. On board is the furniture that didn't fit into the Newport house, which we put into storage. Some of our stuff we sold as we were downsizing from four to three bedrooms. As British houses are smaller than those in Australia, we thought we'd better get used to living with less space.

On our last night in Melbourne, we take up Wendy's suggestion to stay at her Airbnb, which she generously offers us for free. A friend who has lived abroad said it's easy to lose touch when you move and suggested I join Facebook. Wendy finds it easier to keep in touch on the platform than by email. She has documented her illness online to alert others to the symptoms of ovarian cancer and I'm proud to call her my friend. We hug one last time. I have a lump in my throat, but vow not to lose it in front of her.

As we fly out of Tullamarine and on towards a new chapter, I promise to make the most of the opportunities coming my way and not take life for granted.

20

Down Under to Up Over

22 February 2011
In Auckland, the day before we fly to Rarotonga, I use the hotel gym at lunchtime. The television is set to TV One. I take little notice until a news flash catches my eye.

There's been an earthquake in Christchurch.

Christchurch? It's not even on a fault line.

The on-air programme stops, then cuts to a newsreader wearing a dark suit jacket and a sombre-looking tie.

Similar to the obit (obituary) rehearsals we used to do on The Big Breakfast. Only this is for real.

I finish my workout, but stay on the exercise bike, watching the TV. I text BB Lookalike.

"Have you heard about Christchurch?"

"What about it?"

"A big earthquake right in the centre."

"How big?"

"6.3."

"Finishing up here, see you in 10."

We spend the rest of the day glued to the TV, only tearing ourselves away to catch up with friends for an early dinner. Then it's back to the apartment, where I pull everything out of my main suitcase, flatten, roll and squash all my belongings to fit better. I hang my travelling clothes in the bathroom, hoping the steam from the shower will iron out the creases, as Joan Collins promises will happen in an article published in *The Guardian*. It was news to me Dame Joan does her own packing and was happy to write up her advice in a lefty newspaper.

While I concentrate on getting everything into the case, I'm watching the news. There are stories of survivors who ran late and missed their meetings in the collapsed buildings, as well as the tragedies of innocent bystanders who had the misfortune to be in the wrong place at the wrong time.

The following day, we are up at 5am and out the door, waiting for our cab to the airport at 6.15am. By 7.15am, we're checked in. We go through security and grab a coffee and croissant. Breakfast TV covers nothing but the Christchurch earthquake and the aftermath. I will follow up when we return to England to find an appeal to which I can donate.

As we make our way to our aircraft seats, I can't help but admire how comfortable they look.

I ask the flight attendant, 'Have we been upgraded?'

'Yes, you both have. The flight's not full.'

'Wow! This is a good start to our holiday.'

'You're welcome,' she says.

Fewer than four hours later, we land at Rarotonga, where all the passengers are greeted with a garland of flowers. A ukulele player serenades us with a song of two to three lines, which repeatedly contain the words "Rarotonga," "I love you" and "my island home." We jump in a taxi and are driven for a few kilometres to our holiday accommodation, a self-catering cabin on a white sand beach overlooking an idyllic lagoon complete with swaying palm trees. Our next-door neighbours are locals, and their chickens peck away in front of our chalet.

After unpacking, we walk to the local supermarket and buy our supplies. Everyone we speak to has a Kiwi accent.

This place has a South Auckland gone troppo vibe.

We pop our heads into the local fish and chip shop, where the fish comes South Pacific style with chips made out of kumara (sweet potato). Once back at the cabin, we stash our groceries, change into our swimmers, and head down the beach to the lagoon. I wear reef shoes to avoid stepping on the delicate corals. The temperature is 28C, and the water is at least 25C.

We dine out on fresh fish and salads at the local restaurants in the evenings. We take a taxi tour of the island, which takes 45 minutes at a steady 40 kilometres an hour. Our driver points out Rarotonga's best bars and the expensive houses where government ministers live. We go out on a boat across the lagoon and BB Lookalike buys an ill-fitting boatman's hat. The most adventurous we get is kayaking for the first time. We're hopeless and veer from one side to the other until we learn to paddle evenly. After the inevitable mishap tips us into the water, it's easy to get back on again as the lagoon is so shallow.

We watch television for the ads rather than the offerings on the two channels. The ads have all been dubbed with a Cook Islands voiceover, which puts a local spin on big brands such as Coca-Cola. I also love how inventive Cook Islanders are when creating their version of fast food. No KFC? No problem. There's a lady down the road making her own RFC (Rarotonga Fried Chicken). This is a place with secret herbs and spices where 100% of the profits stay on the island instead of going to shareholders overseas.

The five days pass in a blur of sundowners at sunset, gazing up at the stars in skies with no light pollution, the morning wake-up call by the local rooster, and as many kumara chips as two people can eat. Then, we arrange a mini-bus transfer to the airport to catch the weekly direct Air New Zealand flight from Rarotonga to LA.

We'd better not miss it.

On our final evening, the rain lashes down, and we get soaked moving our suitcases from our cabin to the reception area. I amuse myself by having one last watch of the TV ads.

I'm hoping the ten-hour flight will give me time to adjust from the laid-back Southern Hemisphere to the fast-paced Northern, but the holiday ends at the airport. At check-in, representatives of the United States immigration department grill us.

The rain is still lashing down as we take our seats (no upgrade this time). I'm not one for white-knuckle rides, but despite the bad weather, there are only a few bumps as we climb up, up and away.

There can be no greater culture shock than the one we are about to experience when this flight lands. To take my mind off the transit nightmare of LAX, I cheer myself up by watching *Downton Abbey*, the country house drama filmed in Hampshire at a stately home thirty minutes' drive from Winchester. Time passes in a blur. Before I know it, I'm on the last episode, and as I glance out my window, below me are mountains. I pay scant attention to whether they are the Santa Monicas or the San Gabriels as all I care about is will or won't Lady Mary and Matthew the Earl of Grantham get it on?

As the plane stops at the gate, I am slow to remove my headphones.

Showtime.

We shuffle off the plane and make our way through the slow sea of humanity, all trying to retrieve their luggage from the crowded carousel. Once we collect our bags, we amble forward to security screening. In front of us, a group of Canadians are giving a running commentary.

'Look over there,' one guy points out to me. 'It's a weapon,' he says in a stage whisper. 'In Canada, only trained police officers can carry them, not any guy off the street.'

I try to suppress my giggling, but it's too late. A woman in a paramilitary style uniform catches me out and glares at me.

'Shoes off, purse here,' she shouts.

Yes, but we call them handbags. A purse is what you call a wallet. Wonder if she worked in a prison before this job?

BB Lookalike is told to remove his belt.

I hope his trousers stay up.

When I go to the Air New Zealand check-in desk to present my upgrade request, the woman there throws it back, doing her best to laugh as much as her surgically enhanced face and bee-sting lips will allow. She shakes her head.

'No, no, no. Nada. No upgrades on points on this flight,' she sneers. 'No spare seats. Besides, it's awards season.'

There's no need to rub it in. You may wear an Air New Zealand uniform, but your attitude is 100% LA.

As I settle down in my economy seat, I'm looking forward to saying adios to La-La Land and hello to cold rainy England.

21

A Two Pub Village

As the airport doors fly open at Heathrow on the last official day of winter, a gust of wind blows a snowdrift towards us. I leap back. Yes, it's snowing in Middlesex.

A family member is waiting for us in their car, having kindly offered to pick us up. The drive from Heathrow to Winchester takes us an hour and a quarter. I'm excited as we turn off the motorway and follow signs to the city centre. Neither of us has yet set foot in Winchester, but with this move, I've done my homework for once.

It's Lilliput. How do two cars get down a road designed for a horse and carriage?

Our eyelids droop. I don't dare count the number of hours we've been travelling. Our family member drops us off, promising to catch up with us the following weekend. Despite an overwhelming urge to sleep, we resist; it's only four in the afternoon.

Our rented apartment is one of two in a small subdivided Victorian terraced house. It is on the first floor, accessed via steps from the back, and can't be more than 30 square metres. The decor is drab 1980s office—grey industrial carpet, magnolia-coloured walls, and poor-quality furniture. Crammed into the space is a bedroom, bathroom, kitchen, and sitting room.

The landlord must have seen us coming. She's charging us £500 a week for this, but we don't have an alternative.

We unpack, and then explore the town to find the nearest supermarket. By the time we've finished our shopping, it's 5pm, and already the light is fading. Readjusting to the lack of light in the English winter will take some doing, but for now, we are in a no-man's land of jetlag, so it won't matter what time the sun goes down.

The first evening, we cobble a meal together. BB Lookalike stands in the tiny kitchen and I am on the other side of the counter in the sitting room.

How long before cabin fever sets in?

The next morning, we wake early. Our sitting room and kitchen face a busy street on the one-way system, so we know it is commuter time. The upside of this flat is the proximity to Winchester School of Art. It will take BB Lookalike all of one minute to walk to work.

I hit the ground running and spend the morning researching houses and flats to rent. There's very little on offer and all of them say no to pets.

But Britain is supposed to be a nation of animal lovers. Or have I been out of the country for too long?

'Yes, it's true,' an estate agent tells me. 'It's the landlords renting out property who aren't. I have nothing in Winchester now, but how about this?' She turns her screen towards me. It's a three-bedroom house in a nearby village called Easton. 'They'd consider a dog as there's a big back garden.'

'When can I see it?' I say, trying not to sound too excited.

'Let me call them. When suits?' I recall BB Lookalike's

schedule, which he mentioned in passing. I think he said he's free on Friday.

'Friday, in the morning?'

'It suits them. They're packing up to leave in a couple of weeks, so I hope you don't mind there will be boxes everywhere.'

'No, I don't mind at all.'

I hope no one else with a dog sees it before we do.

By Thursday, BB Lookalike and I are tripping over each other in the tiny flat. Friday can't come soon enough.

Winchester is Toy Town compared with the wide open spaces of Australia. I'm walking down North Walls on the narrow pavement, trying to pass another pedestrian. As I squeeze by, a coach comes thundering down the left-hand lane next to me. I'm on the edge of the footpath, and as I step aside to avoid the pedestrian, I feel a whoosh of air. The coach's massive side mirror takes up so much space, it protrudes across my path millimetres from my head. It's bad enough being a pedestrian, how am I going to cope with driving on these tiny roads?

I'm putting off buying a car until we've found a place to live. And wherever it is, it must be commutable for BB Lookalike, who intends to walk or cycle to work. Easton fits the bill, although it's cut off by the motorway and has no bus service.

I plan a scenic walk to our viewing on Friday. It's on a well-mapped footpath, and the route takes us across water meadows, beside the river, and over fields. Winchester became a city because of its cathedral, but the centre is compact and it has a population of only 48,000. In fewer

The Accidental Plus One

than fifteen minutes, we've left it behind and are walking along the River Itchen in the countryside. The path bends its way underneath the A34, and once through the underpass, we cross a stile and are in lush fields, where the only sound is the rhythmic munching of cattle grazing.

From this angle, the view is timeless. The tallest building is the church spire in the next village, which must be Easton. A handsome Georgian house comes into view. As the Australians might say, it's as if we've walked onto the set of a bonnet drama. We climb over another stile and carry on straight down into the village. In front of us is a pub, the Cricketers Inn.

'I can stop off here for a pint on the way home,' BB Lookalike says. We pace out 50 steps from the pub to the house we're here to view.

The house is a semi-detached brick building, constructed in the 1960s, I guess, but with new double-glazed windows. It has a bonus downstairs cloakroom, a spacious modern kitchen, and an open-plan dining/sitting room facing south and west to the sizeable garden laid to lawn. Upstairs are three bedrooms, one large and two smaller.

'We'd love to put in an application,' I say to the owner's father, who has shown us the house. I show him a photo of Zebedee. 'This is our Labrador. She'd love the garden. She's in Devon, staying with family until we can find a house to rent.'

As we head down past the pub, we observe practically every other house features a thatched roof, reminiscent of the cottages seen in calendars of "Olde England." Round the corner, we walk past a barn and a farm on the right. There in front of us is another pub, The Chestnut Horse, decorated with hanging baskets and planter boxes brimming with purple pansies and crimson geraniums. I peruse the menu, pinned up on a board outside. It's my kind of food—a modern take on British classics with local ingredients.

'This one looks more my style,' I say. 'But two pubs in one village? I don't think we'd find better than this. Let's ring the agent.' Without hesitation, I do so. 'We're walking back from Easton, checking out the cycle path under the motorway. So we'll come straight to you to sort out the paperwork and see you in about an hour,' I tell her.

Our route takes us up Easton Lane, which is a steep but picturesque walk. The road is so narrow, it is a single lane, with passing bays for cars to pull over. Luckily, no cars go by, and as we reach the brow of the hill, we work out why. There is an intersection with another single-track lane, but then Easton Lane turns into a bike route as it heads up towards the underpass of the motorway. Perfect for cyclists and walkers, as there can't be many vehicles going up and down here. There are only two farms and a half-dozen houses.

The owners of the Easton house are away on secondment in the USA and are planning to rent it out for a year and see what happens afterwards. A year is perfect as this allows us time to look for somewhere to buy. They have accepted our application for the house. We've only been in Winchester four days, and already, we've found somewhere to live. What good luck.

As all our worldly goods are on the high seas, it will be another three weeks before we can move. I can't wait to get out of the tiny apartment, as the landlord, who also owns the downstairs flat, has the builders in for the next two weeks.

"It's a shame you forgot to tell us you were renovating. If we'd known, we'd have gone elsewhere."

The landlord ignores my emails.

I plan to spend as much time outside the apartment as possible and write in the library and cafes if necessary. Now we have an official new address, I join the local gym and sign up for group exercise classes. And I buy an estate car, which is handy for carting our stuff from the apartment to the new house.

To minimise the stress, I wait until we have moved in before driving down to Devon to pick up Zebedee. I needn't have worried. She loves her new digs. And being a water dog, she loves the River Itchen and all the ducks.

One of the first things we do is ask if we can plant a vegetable garden as the lawn slopes down and gets all-day sun. The landlords agree, as we will pay a gardener to dig out a suitable area and plant it. And on their return, they will benefit from having a ready-made vegetable plot. Our next-door neighbour, who must be in his eighties, spends all day in his vegetable garden and will teach me what to plant and how to look after what I grow. I'm so keen to do this, I make the rookie error of buying four courgette plants, which give us a glut of vegetables.

I can't help thinking the landlords in Winchester who didn't want to take a dog did us a favour. We love living in the village, and the house suits us well. The Itchen Valley is a hidden gem and a favourite haunt for cyclists and walkers. Its most famous resident was Charles Kingsley who was inspired by the river to dream up *The Water Babies*, the book about Tom the chimney sweep that had me in floods of tears as a child.

Although BB Lookalike does drop into the Cricketers

on his way home to have a pint and do some writing, he soon takes to drinking in the Chestnut Horse, along with all the other men in the village. I catch them out one evening, sitting in the bar, in thrall to Lauren, the landlady, who could have been a model in another life.

I glance over to the stone floor, where a motley assortment of bored dogs take turns to sigh.

I bet these men told their other halves they were taking the dog out for a walk.

I sit myself up at the bar, unable to contain my amusement.

'I'll have a sauvignon blanc, thanks, Lauren.'

As summer gives way to autumn, we have settled into life in the bucolic countryside. It's early September, and the fields are glowing in the light unique to that time of year when I get a phone call from the letting agent.

'I have bad news, I'm afraid. Your landlords want to break the lease after nine months.'

'Oh no. That means we have to be out at the end of December.' We have a family Christmas arranged, and although they'll all be gone by then, it's going to be a pain to pack up and find movers during the Silly Season.

'They're coming back early because the wife is pregnant and they want to have the baby in England rather than America.'

'Will they allow us to stay until mid-January, given everything shuts down over Christmas?'

'That seems fair enough.'

'Thanks for letting me know.'

With a heavy heart, I call BB Lookalike and tell him the saga. 'I'm looking at houses to buy,' I say. 'Shall we sound out the landlords to see whether they'd sell? Then we wouldn't have to move again.'

'They can only say no.'

The Accidental Plus One

The husband is keen, but his wife isn't.

We have no desire to leave Easton, but it's tiny and tightly held. People don't need to put houses on the open market here; they are snapped up through word-of-mouth. I ask Lauren to let me know if she hears about anything suitable coming up. But I'm forced to look elsewhere as we have a deadline.

I spend September trawling the internet, looking for suitable houses. I try Hyde near the gym, but the houses are too small and the gardens even smaller. I'm keen on a house which needs a major renovation, but BB Lookalike hates it. He wants a finished house to move into while I want a project.

We put in an offer on a three-bedroom mid-terrace in St Cross near the water meadows. It's owned by an architect, and there's not one bit of wasted space. She's even crammed in a tiny cloakroom under the stairs, which impresses me. Our offer is rejected, and I'm relieved. There's no access from the back, and we'd be wheeling our bikes and the bins through the house onto the street.

'I want a house I can walk around,' BB Lookalike tells me. Even though it's my turn to choose, I agree.

'Terraces are out then, so it's semis or detached houses,' I say.

I widen my search to include two-bedroom houses and find a brand-new semi in a small development south of Winchester, at the end of a dead-end road which turns into a bridleway. It has the same footprint as a three-bedder, but the developer was told by the council that the development needed some affordable homes and he had to make it two, not three. He turned the third bedroom into an extra bathroom, making it ideal for guests. It's set in a good-sized front garden with mature trees and hedges.

You'd never know it was a new build.

The agent is waiting outside for me. He pushes the double-glazed front door open, leading me into a porch suitable for boots and shoes. Then a second double-glazed door opens onto a wide square hallway.

Somewhere for all the books.

And a handy downstairs cloakroom on the left of the hallway.

A door from the hallway opens up into the open-plan living area. There is a compact L-shaped kitchen, well-designed to save space. It has shaker-style units painted in a soft pale green with pale beech worktops. A Belfast sink completes the look.

The entire ground floor is laid with wood flooring. Doors from the dining area lead out onto a south-facing paved patio. Behind the kitchen is a compact back garden, big enough for a raised bed, a barbecue, and a small shed. In my head, I've already bought this house, and I haven't seen the upstairs yet.

There's still work to be done as there's no stairway carpet and the upstairs floors need to be laid. But as I walk into the huge main bedroom, I picture myself waking up here, looking up through the skylights. It's full of light, even though it's autumn.

The original plan for the large en-suite bathroom, which leads off the master bedroom, was for it to be the third bedroom. The other bedroom is right next door and is much smaller, but it still has space for a queen-sized bed and fitted cupboards. Next to it is the second bathroom, which was the only one in the original design.

I'm impressed by the high-quality fixtures and fittings including travertine tiles and wooden double-glazed windows. Even the door furniture is attractive. I call BB Lookalike and tell him he needs to get here as soon as he can. He says he can nip out at lunchtime. Two hours later, we are back, and both agree this is the house for us.

'Even though this village has neither a shop nor a pub?'

'Let's take a drive,' BB Lookalike suggests.

There's a pub in the next village, within twenty minutes' walk, right beside the local railway station with direct connections to Southampton, London, and all the stops in between. On the weekend, we time the walk to the station and stop in at the pub for lunch. The beer meets with BB Lookalike's approval and the food is decent.

'Shall we give this one a go, then?'

'Yes.'

Before I make the offer, I do my due diligence on the development. This is one of six houses the developer built, and he has yet to sell any of them. The other houses, apart from next door, are all detached and three times the size, so will take longer to sell. The developer's timing was off as he completed the houses when the market was in the doldrums.

'I'm going to make a cheeky offer. And see what happens.' My offer is £20,000 below the asking price. We still have to carpet the stairs, lay wooden floors in both bedrooms, fit wardrobes, and put in blinds and shutters throughout. This will swallow up the £20,000 we hope to save on the asking price.

The developer doesn't quibble and accepts.

My hunch must have been correct.

What my due diligence didn't factor in is the hostility from the locals, many of whom campaigned to stop our development from being built. Shortly after moving in, we are chopping back our hedge when a passer-by yells at us.

'You can't cut that. It's listed.'

'Not according to the plans,' I reply as BB Lookalike continues chopping. The man harrumphs and walks off, muttering. We hear the word "Australian," or as he pronounces it, "Orstrylian." So from now on, we are known as the "Orstrylians."

We can't win. In Lancashire, we were "them southerners."

22

The Pilgrims' Way

To reconnect with Britain, BB Lookalike suggests we go on a walk. A long one—the 119-mile Pilgrims' Way between Winchester and Canterbury.

Can't we experience this vicariously, reading up on it from a warm, cosy pub?

Nope, we're going for the full immersive experience—hiking ancient bridleways, woodlands, uplands and downlands. We ask friends and family if they'd be interested in joining us. And soon, we are a group of six, including a dog.

Someone suggests we ask the Bishops of Winchester and Canterbury for a blessing. BB Lookalike and I are doing this walk for secular rather than religious reasons. We are not walking, as 12th-century pilgrims did, to pay our respects to Thomas Becket, Archbishop of Canterbury, who was murdered in 1170 at the behest of Henry II. But we're happy to go along with the plan.

Sadly, Zebedee is too old for this walk, and taking her place is a young, active male black Labrador. Zebedee is recovering from illness on the first day of the walk, so I volunteer to be the designated driver, carrying the luggage to each new destination. Her dog sitters, a delightful couple in their nineties, are still game to look after her.

The heavens open when the pilgrims set off from Winchester Cathedral. And to add to their misery, the Bishop of Winchester gives them short shrift and declines to bless them.

Not very Christian.

The next day, I put Zebedee, her dog bed and food in the car, and drive her down to the south coast to the dog sitters. Then it's off to the bed-and-breakfast where the walkers stayed the night to collect the luggage, ferrying it on to the next overnight stop in Farnham where I'll meet up with the pilgrims. Our generous hosts there have the five of us plus one dog to stay, and ply us with drinks, dinner, and breakfast the following day.

I walk halfway with the group, then turn back the way we've come, collect the car and drive the bags to stop number three, between Guildford and Dorking. At the end of this day, we say goodbye to one walker who goes home to recuperate from painful blisters.

We stay the night at a hotel, and the following day, I pack up the bags to take to the next stop for the night, a detour to a Premier Inn on the M25 London Orbital road, the only dog-friendly accommodation we could find. Despite the location near a busy motorway, the hotel is triple-glazed, and we get a quiet night's sleep at a very reasonable price.

The next day, I pack the car with the bags and the passengers, and drop the walkers off at the North Downs. Then I leave the car at the next accommodation and join them halfway in the North Weald of Kent. It doesn't take long to slip into the rhythm of putting one foot in front of the other and immersing myself in the moment as I

The Accidental Plus One

contemplate how many feet have trodden this path over the centuries.

We walk over hills, across lush green grass in open countryside, through wooded copses. Up here in the Weald, we hear birdsong and the occasional tractor. It's another world away from the busy A2/M2 motorway connecting London to the Channel ports. Waiting for us as we roll into our stop for the last night of this epic journey is the missing member of our group, rested up and intent on completing the walk.

The following morning, fortified by a cooked breakfast, we set off on what promises to be a glorious summer's day. I load up the car as we will return here from Canterbury by taxi at the end of the walk.

Not long after we leave the idyllic little village, the North Downs Way takes us past a house next to the path, from where a team of crime scene investigators dressed in paper overalls, plastic overshoes, face masks, and gloves emerges. My knee-jerk reaction is to look for a camera crew. Have we stumbled upon a location shoot for a crime drama? But it's real-life, not fiction, and we're witnessing the work of actual CSIs going about their day job.

I try not to speculate about what we've seen and concentrate on the track ahead. From 11 kilometres/8 miles away, we spy Canterbury Cathedral. I've only walked part of the route, but it still feels epic.

We stumble upon No Man's Community Orchard in Chartham. Now a protected nature reserve, it contains a serpent seat sculpture, where we stop to rest and take in the beauty of our surroundings. Each family in this community has their own Bramley apple tree, from which they can pick the fruit.

When we arrive at Canterbury Cathedral, a member of the clergy greets us as we have pre-arranged our visit.

We spot her by her clerical shirt and collar, which she pairs with regular clothing.

'Welcome, pilgrims,' she says, bending down to say hello to the Labrador. He has his tongue lolling out, greeting her with a sloppy kiss. She doesn't so much as flinch. 'Come with me, all of you,' she says, gazing down at the dog.

She sets off at a pace, and we rush to keep up. We must look a sight, the five of us and one four-legged companion basking in the attention. She hurries us along the long corridors where we pass more senior clergy, who give us disapproving looks. Our saviour puts up her hand as soon as one goes to open his mouth.

'It's all right,' she says. 'All under control.'

We follow her down the steps and into the crypt. 'Gather round,' she instructs. Even the dog has grasped the solemnity of this occasion and he sits down, sensing something is about to happen. And indeed, it does.

Not only have BB Lookalike and I reconnected with family and the ancient byways of Britain, we've been blessed at the country's pre-eminent cathedral, which has stood on this site since 597AD.

Our route took us away from the Kent coast, but if it hadn't and the conditions had been right, we'd have been able to see France, the gateway to Europe. And we can't wait to explore it.

By now, it's late 2013, and BB Lookalike has moved universities and works at the place he has always aspired to —an art school that's part of the University of London. He commutes from our nearest railway station, which is walkable, one of the reasons we bought our house.

The Accidental Plus One

The Sorbonne in Paris has extended an invitation for him to lecture, a prestigious gig if ever there was one. But its budget for visiting speakers is minuscule, and the accommodation is a night in a two-star hotel.

Are they having a laugh?

I still go; it's Paris, after all. It takes my mind off the tough decision we had to make in the late summer when the vet took me aside and said Zebedee, who was fifteen, had a poor quality of life as she was by then deaf and partially sighted, and increasingly suffering from spinal stenosis. This was the last thing I wanted to hear, but as hard as it was for me, it was harder to tell BB Lookalike. She'd lived longer than any of the dogs I grew up with, but it didn't make the decision any easier.

The vet and nurse came to our house, and we sat under Zebedee's favourite tree. As we watched her fall asleep and slip away, the veterinary nurse couldn't hold back her tears. And neither could we. Zebedee was more than a dog; she was part of our family and the grieving process would be a long one.

I throw myself into travelling as the accidental plus one, relishing the novelty of Europe on our doorstep—so close, it's quicker to go by train than to fly. In our hotel in Paris, the walls are paper thin, and we can hear every word of the phone conversation going on in the next room.

Is he talking about Sartre, Proust, or existentialism?

Is he heck. BB Lookalike says the guest in the neighbouring room is talking about widgets. How many and when should they be delivered?

I accompany BB Lookalike on two work trips to Rome, which I use for research for *Nighthawks*, a thriller about looted art and the second Stephen Connor mystery written under our Lambert Nagle pen name. But the strangest trips of all are to Austria.

23

The Hills are Alive

If I'd known Arnold Schwarzenegger's former home was a museum in Graz, I'd have gone there instead of the art gallery. I'm the only visitor.

It's Saturday. Where is everybody?

I buy my ticket from the young woman behind the desk, who seems friendly. Then I browse, stopping at the various paintings and sculptures to read the descriptions, which are in English and German. But as I peer at the exhibits, I notice a shadow behind me. A person-shaped one.

I glance back. It's the young woman who sold me my ticket.

'Hi,' I say. 'Is everything okay?'

'No. Not really.'

I turn towards her. 'Oh dear, did I not pay the right amount?'

'It is your bag.' She is now so close, I can hear her breathe.

What does she think is in there? Weapons?

'I enjoy going to galleries,' I say pointedly. 'But I'm not

enjoying this one. As I'm being tailed.'

'You have a rucksack,' the young woman says in a disapproving tone. I take off my bag, which has two straps and can be worn either front or back, and do my best catwalk twirl, minus the swagger and scowl.

'Not so much a rucksack as a versatile handbag.' I sling it over one shoulder using a single strap. 'Now it's an ordinary handbag.'

She shrugs, unimpressed. 'All rucksacks must be checked in.' She reminds me of an argumentative European colleague I worked with at Disney.

'You're welcome to see inside. See, nothing in there.' Then I go in for my parting shot. 'You didn't mention this when I bought my ticket.'

She averts her gaze.

Got you there.

I carry on, but mirroring my every move, three paces behind me, is the shadow. I turn to face her again.

'You're not busy serving anyone else, then?'

'No.'

I glance at the empty gallery. 'Maybe no one wants to come here because they find it creepy to be followed.'

Another shrug.

'I can't concentrate on the artwork with you following my every move, so I'm going to go now. Bye.'

I walk out of the deserted gallery. And unlike Arnie, I won't be back.

I hope for better luck on my next jaunt, which is to Piber, the historic breeding and training complex for the Lipizzaner horses of the Spanish Riding School. The breed, one of the oldest in Europe, has existed since the 16th century. It seems rude not to visit while I have the chance.

The journey involves a train, a bus, and donning my walking shoes. I buy my ticket from the Graz Main Station machine and work out I'll need to change at Köflach for the bus to Piber. As I'm sitting on the train, there's an announcement. I only know the words for train station, airport, eggs, and please, excuse me and thank you in German. And it's bound to be bad news—a delay or a rail replacement bus. I look for someone who might speak English. A young student, seventeen or maybe eighteen, is my pick.

'*Entschuldigung, bitter. Sprechen English?*' I say.

'Yes, a little,' she says.

'What was the announcement?'

'We must get out two stops before Köflach and then travel by bus.'

'I'm trying to get to Piber.'

'You must make the change and then get on the Piber bus. I can show you if you follow me.'

Then we start chatting about Graz versus where I live. My new best friend finds it astonishing a city the size of Winchester lacks an opera house. I do my best to sell it.

'There's a theatre and a 10th-century cathedral,' I venture.

'What is the population of Winchester? Graz has 283,000 people.'

'I'm not sure. Let me look it up. Here it is: 124,000 if you include the surrounding villages, but 48,000 in the city centre.'

'There are many smaller cities in Austria which will have an opera company, even if they do not have an opera house,' she says.

Graz un point, Winchester nil points.

The Accidental Plus One

Still, I'm grateful, as without her help, I'd be stuck on Platform 9.

My next challenge is to ask the bus driver to drop me off at Piber. When my young friend gets off, I approach him.

'Piber, *danke*,' I say.

'Ja, ja.' He nods and points up front. The bus slows down as we roll into town. There's not much to it, and this being Sunday, nothing stirs. Austria must be similar to Germany, as it appears to be closed for business on the Lord's Day.

Are all 500 inhabitants at church?

I printed off a paper map for the last part of my journey and according to this, I need to trek up a hill. Walking up the slope beside what I'd call an A road, I've been going ten minutes before I even see a car. From every angle is a picture-perfect alpine landscape—a calendar vista. As I look out over the hills and valleys, there is no trace of the modern world. Wildflowers, including poppies in every hue, dot the lush green fields. I catch myself humming *Edelweiss*.

I bet the cows in the meadow are wearing collars with bells.

As you have probably guessed, *The Sound of Music* was my favourite film when I was small.

'When I grow up, I want to be Maria,' I declared back then. Two and a half years later, I met actual nuns at boarding school. With one notable exception, they were ancient and incapable of running for a bus, let alone down a hillside, arms spread out, singing the opening song from the movie.

Up ahead is a pointy wooden church, and out of it spills an animated group of families dressed up in traditional costumes. Linking arms, they come hurtling towards me. The men are in Lederhosen and Tyrolean hats. The women wear wide skirts and fitted bodices, some more revealing than others. Whatever the occasion, it looked like it was going to be fun.

After another 500 metres, I spy a big mansion. Once the Abbey of St Lambrecht, Piber Castle is no longer home to ladies, lords, or monks, but is now a stud farm for horses. In times past, they were beasts of burden—war horses carrying the gentry into battle. I queue up at the gate and pay my money, then at last, I'm let loose in amongst all these photogenic equines. The staff makes sure we visitors are kept at a distance from the nursery, where white mares tenderly nuzzle their offspring as the dark bay foals suckle from them.

I tag on to a tour, not because I can understand the German commentary, but for the chance to ogle more horses. In one stall is a majestic-looking stallion, kept in splendid isolation, whinnying and mane-tossing to all the mares. By the looks of him, he's keen to sire more progeny —unsuitable for Sunday afternoon family viewing, so the poor fellow must wait until we've all gone.

I lose count of the horses I've seen today as I go back down the hill to the bus stop and wait. The opulent surroundings in which they live are astounding. But I find out later it's a miracle the breed survived at all. In World War II, the Germans evacuated the horses to Czechoslovakia. But in 1945, after the Nazis surrendered, the horses were in danger of being devoured by a hungry Soviet army. News of the horses' plight reached the highest ranks of the United States Army. "Operation Cowboy," on the orders of General S Patton, saved 1,200 horses, including 400 Lipizzaners. US Army officers who were also experienced horsemen rode, trucked, and herded them across the German border to safety. In 1952, the Lipizzaners moved to Piber, where they have lived in peace in their castle ever since.

BB Lookalike receives an invitation to a conference about media, the environment, and mountains, which is a perfect fit for the venue in Innsbruck. This will be my third visit to Austria, and I'm excited to go to the mountains, especially because *Spectre*, my favourite James Bond movie, was filmed near Innsbruck.

We arrive in Munich at 2pm after our flight from Heathrow. By 2.30pm, we have collected our luggage and contact Hans from Tyrolean Travel, who will drive us on the shuttle service 200 kilometres to Innsbruck. A mild-looking man in his fifties, with thinning grey hair and standard-issue glasses, Hans speaks English with a distinct accent.

'I lived in Manchester for three years in the 90s.'

'Your accent is a bit of a giveaway.'

He grins, puffing himself up. 'They were good times,' he reflects, then flicks back to driver mode. 'I have a few more passengers to find,' he says, walking off.

We sit in the arrivals area with our luggage. The shuttle bus company promises Security. Reliability. Comfort. What we get when we board the minibus ten minutes later is Hans's favourite music. First up are The Rolling Stones with *It's Only Rock 'n' Roll (But I Like It)*, followed by The Beatles. Most of the people on the bus are too young to know either band.

Hans didn't get into the Madchester music scene, then. No Happy Mondays, Inspiral Carpets or even Oasis.

I look out the window, disappointed at the scenery. I'm hoping for spectacular mountains, but the journey so far has been motorways and tunnels. We're still chugging along the motorway when we see them—the mountains are indeed spectacularly jagged and pointy.

Hans indicates and pulls off the highway.

'Passenger for Ebbs,' he calls out. A woman in the front row of seats nods. The village is small and cute, with the kind of scenery you'd find on a biscuit tin. Wooden chalets with window boxes dot the hills. We pull up in the forecourt of a service station, where the driver hands the woman her suitcase, and she trots off and into a waiting taxi.

We set off again to Guns N' Roses *Sweet Child of Mine*, a song I have heard at the gym far too many times. Fortunately, the next stop isn't too far away, where Hans fuels up. From the original eight passengers, we're now four. The two of us plus a man in his forties in a Marks & Spencer type suit and a glamorous twenty-something with lips that make her look like a startled duck.

You'd think all that filler might make her trip over her words.

But nope, she keeps up her non-stop phone conversation in Spanish for a good hour, without so much as a lisp.

With an hour to go, Hans makes one more stop before Innsbruck and deposits the man in the suit into the middle of nowhere. And then, it's only us and Duckface left. Hans attempts conversation with BB Lookalike and me, because his other passenger is still yacking away into her phone.

'You know, Donald Trump is the true saviour of the world.'

BB Lookalike and I give each other the side-eye, trying not to make it too obvious in case Hans can read the room. I grab my phone.[1]

'In what way?' I say, poised to take notes.

'He's battling to expose all the paedophiles in the Democrat party.'

'Paedophiles?'

'A Satan-worshipping child-sex ring that has control of the media and politics is at the heart of the Democrat party. Donald Trump is the one true saviour, telling the truth.'

We reach the outskirts of Innsbruck, and I'm hoping we aren't about to be dropped off, as I can't wait to hear the next instalment. Luckily, Hans takes a right, and we climb a steep hill away from the town centre. Duckface, still with the phone glued to her ear, grabs her things. Hans gets out and hands her an enormous plasticky suitcase with Louis Vuitton logos splashed all over it.

Fake lips and matching fake luggage.

I cut to the chase as soon as Hans hops back into the van.

'Which Democrats in particular?'

'Every single top one you can think of: Hillary Clinton, Barack Obama and George Soros. Then there's the Hollywood celebrities: Tom Hanks... and Oprah.'

'Tom Hanks and Oprah are involved in this?'

'Yep. And you wouldn't believe who else.'

Go on, try me.

'The Pope and the Dalai Lama.' Hans is on a roll now. 'Have you heard of adrenochrome?'

'No, I haven't heard of it.'

'What about the lizard people?'

'Nor them either.'

I shift about in my seat, now keen to escape. Hans drives us down the hill and into town, to my great relief. As he pulls up outside Hotel Innsbruck and we unload our bags, I can't help but wonder what led him down the rabbit hole.

'Bye, Hans, thanks for getting us here in one piece,' I say.

'I enjoyed talking with you. Do your own research on adrenochrome and the lizard people, won't you?' Hans says, waving goodbye.

'We will.'

I feel sorry Hans believes in these conspiracy theories, but I'm glad to see the back of him. When I go online and "do my own research," I find out he has been regurgitating falsehoods going back to the nineteenth century.

When we order our taxi at the end of the Moving Mountains conference, I turn to BB Lookalike.

'I'm hoping our driver won't have time to tell us what he thinks about the world, given we're flying out of Innsbruck and the airport is pretty close.'

'With any luck,' says BB Lookalike.

It's a great relief when this taxi driver keeps his thoughts and fears to himself, even if he does believe a genetically modified half-human half-lizard race known as the "Babylonian Brotherhood" is out to create a worldwide state.

[1] Hans's conspiracy theories inspired the character Paolo, an antiquities looter, in *Nighthawks* by Lambert Nagle. (See the Also By section for the link to this book.)

24

East in Sweden

'Wouldn't it be fun to cultivate some contacts in tropical places?' I say to BB Lookalike. 'I hear the Caribbean is lovely at this time of year.'

'They can't afford to pay airfares or visiting speakers.'

Oh well, I tried.

The most generous institutions are in cities in cold places, rather than flop and drop seaside resorts.

'How about Sweden? I've had an invitation to give a seminar at the University of Umeå.'

'Hang on, let me look it up,' I say, grabbing my phone and googling. 'Umeå in northern Sweden. Birthplace of Stieg Larsson. As I loved *The Girl with the Dragon Tattoo*, it's a yes from me.'

Our flight from the UK will land in Stockholm, where Larsson's *Millennium* trilogy is set. We plan to squeeze in a weekend break first, before travelling up to Umeå on Monday.

We depart Heathrow on Saturday 3 October 2015 at 7am after spending Friday night at the Hilton Garden Inn, a five-minute journey to Terminal 2 via a covered walkway.

The flight is two and a half hours, and we arrive in Stockholm at 10.30am local time. It's 12C, but the sun is out, and it's forecasted to be 15C and sunny all day.

We are staying at the Story Hotel at Riddargatan 6 in Östermalm, right in the centre. It's far too early to check in, but the concierge lets us drop our bags off. We wander through Östermalm Market Hall, the food market, where we grab a seafood lunch of juicy prawns, rye bread and beetroot salad. The rest of the day we spend walking through Gamla Stan, the old town which is on one of Stockholm's fourteen islands, as well as going on our own impromptu *Millennium* Trilogy walking tour. And on Sunday, we do a circuit of the Royal National City Park, a 12km loop encircling this beautiful city.

On Monday 5 October, we take the early morning train from Central Station to Umeå. It's 13C when we set off. Umeå is 600 kilometres north of Stockholm and 400km south of the Arctic Circle, so we expect it to be cold. But how cold we're yet to find out.

Umeå is the same distance from Stockholm as Carlisle is to London, and the train fares are almost identical, £100 for a one-way journey. It will take twice as long for us to get there, as up in the remote north there are still single-track lines.

Once we leave Stockholm, we see farms and cultivated land with houses painted in the distinctive Swedish falu red dotting the countryside. As the journey continues north, the landscape changes to vast tracts of forest with several tree species. The only two I can make out are fir and birch.

The route takes us past lakes, and we get tantalising glimpses of log cabins in the woods, which are the stuff of the Scandinavian crime thrillers I devour. You know the sort of thing: a woman is in peril, targeted by a killer in Stockholm or Malmö. The police recommend she move to a safe house. They choose a remote area with only one road in and out. The log cabin has no curtains. At night, the woman sits in a brightly lit room where anyone approaching the cabin can see her. The police mount a 24-hour guard on the property, but there is only one cop at a time on shift, and it's always a rookie recruit.

The serial killer finds out where the woman is and goes after her. He creeps up on the cop outside the cabin and kills him. The woman hears the gunshot and runs out of the back of the cabin, stumbling across the snow towards safety, a main road, anywhere she can. The hero cop finds out she is no longer safe and races against time to save her before the killer gets there first.

If you believed everything about the Sweden of crime thrillers, you'd be too terrified to sleep at night in this country. But it feels very safe to us.

We spot the Höga Kusten (High Coast) Bridge four hours into our trip, close to the village of Veda and spanning the Ångermanälven River. The bridge is 2 kilometres long, about the same length as the Golden Gate Bridge in San Francisco. But despite this spectacular feat of engineering, the train infrastructure still has some catching up to do, as we are soon to find out.

'Ladies and gentlemen, girls and boys. The train in front of us is stuck, and we can't move until the problem is fixed. I am very sorry for the delay to your journey,' our conductor says. Her blonde hair, cut into a short bob, doesn't move as she strides towards us, apologising to all the passengers as we come to a screeching halt.

We sit for an hour waiting for the line to clear, but we don't mind as we aren't in a hurry. Luckily, there is an onboard bistro serving decent sandwiches and various drinks.

Once the track is cleared, we resume our journey and

arrive in Umeå at 5pm. As we get off the train, we're hit by a cold blast of air. I check the temperature. It's a nippy 5C. We cross the road from the railway station and make our way on foot to our hotel, the Winn. It is 400 metres along a flat road and takes fewer than 10 minutes.

The hotel is part of a chain, which is surprising as this outpost has funky decor and bright colours. It's the tallest building in the area with 12 floors, and our room is on the 11th. Our headboard is bright orange, the door to the bathroom is hot neon pink, the bedspread and two chairs are purple, and our combined bedroom and sitting room is the size of a spacious apartment. We sit and watch the sun go down before 6pm, then we head downstairs for a pre-dinner drink and a meal in the hotel.

On Tuesday morning, we have breakfast before setting off on foot to the university campus. I need to find out where it is as I'm due there at 4pm. I'm meeting Brigitta, a lecturer who, as well as a job as a full-time academic, has a side-hustle running a horse trekking centre in the countryside.

Brigitta has offered me a lift to the trekking centre. We will be riding Icelandic ponies, which will be a novelty for me. It's a 20-minute drive.

We change into our riding gear and head out to the stables. The pony I am riding is called Glamur, which translates as Charming. He is a strawberry roan with a ginger forelock, fitting for a Viking horse. I tack him up, and once we're done, Brigitta and I head out of the yard and into the forest.

It's minus 7 degrees C, and I'm feeling the cold. The light is fading, and as we head out, I'm nervous about what we might encounter in this remote forest. I imagine wolves at the very least, and bears.

Brigitta reassures me these ponies are very sure-footed and are shod with shoes designed to grip on snow. The unique selling point of the Icelandic pony is their gait. They have an intermediate speed between walking and trotting, known as "tolting" or tilting.

'Are you ready to try the tolt?' Brigitta asks.

As ready as I'll ever be.

'Okay,' I say. As the wind whips my answer away, Glamur is firing on all four cylinders and moving at the speed of a pocket rocket. We weave in and out of the trees along the forest path, going uphill and downhill at lightning speed. It's a four-beat gait, which is peculiar to observe, but even more peculiar to ride. He's sliding along without a care in the world.

I defy any bear to keep up with this little fellow.

He's on auto-pilot. He's done this many times, even if I haven't. I put all my faith into my sure-footed equine friend and do my best not to unbalance him. And if something untoward happens, I don't have far to fall.

Our exhilarating ride lasts over an hour, and the sun is going down by the time we get back. We untack the ponies and rub them down before putting on their rugs. The sweet smell of pony sweat mingles with the dusty odour of hay. I give Glamur a pat and say *tack* to him, as I don't expect him to understand the English word "thanks." He peers at me through his pale eyelashes.

Sweet.

I plant a kiss on his muzzle. He moves his head back in surprise.

Maybe they aren't soppy about horses here.

I help Brigitta top up the hay nets and the ponies' water. As we leave the barn, we hear the satisfying chomp,

chomp, chomp of blunt pony teeth grinding their way through the hay.

Brigitta ushers me into her warm and cosy retro kitchen, decorated in a cheerful primrose yellow. The bench tops are wooden, and there's an old-fashioned white enamel electric stove. She makes coffee in an Italian stovetop espresso machine identical to the one we have at home. Then she gets out some crispbread and butter and offers me a snack. By now, it is 6.30pm. I warned BB Lookalike not to expect me before eight. I'm hoping there will still be somewhere open for dinner then. People eat early in rural Scandinavia, something I discovered when working in Norway.

'After coffee, I have to go to the supermarket, which isn't far,' Brigitta says. 'And the bus stop for Umeå is opposite. I can drop you off.' It's well below freezing, pitch dark, and we're in the middle of nowhere. Here I am, a total stranger in Brigitta's house. If this was a Swedish crime thriller, I would probably be a serial killer.

'How kind of you. I'll treasure the memory of our ride through the forest.'

'You are very welcome,' Brigitta says, looking a little embarrassed. I guess it's not the Swedish way to be over enthusiastic, but I'm relieved I didn't get chased by a wolf or end up slamming into a fir tree.

Brigitta drives along a lonely road for fifteen minutes and pulls up outside a small supermarket, the Swedish version of a Spar grocery shop. A man is begging in the doorway. Brigitta shakes her head.

'It upsets me to think we have homeless people here now. I want to help them. Can I buy you something to eat?' she asks the man, speaking in English. He looks up at her.

'Hotdog?' he says.

'Okay. Anything to drink?'
'Coffee?'
Brigitta turns towards me.

'If you cross the street, the bus stop is right there.' I look over to where she is pointing. A dozen people are waiting, so the bus must be coming along soon.

'Thanks again, Brigitta,' I call as I walk across the road, my breath visible in the cold, still night.

By the looks of the crowd waiting to get on the bus, they're students on a night out. They're in leggings, jumpers, hats and scarves—not party gear. Umeå doesn't come across as a clubbing hotspot, but as it's one of the few towns before you reach the Arctic Circle 400 kilometres away, this is as good as it will get.

Does the bus run all night? Or will they crash at a friend's place as I used to do when I was their age?

These thoughts run through my head as the bus carries us back along the deserted road to Umeå.

25

The Iron Curtain

I'm gripped by *Deutschland 83*, a TV drama series set at the height of the Cold War. It's an irreverent and insightful coming-of-age story about a young, naïve East German who is forced to spy for the Stasi. So when BB Lookalike accepts an invitation to be the keynote speaker at a conference at the University of Potsdam in July 2016, I'm in. Potsdam, 35km south of Berlin, became part of East Germany when the country was carved up in 1949 by the Soviets.

I went behind the Iron Curtain in the 1980s when I visited West Berlin one Christmas. I started my journey in Florence, travelling overnight to arrive in Munich, from where it was a six-hour train ride to Berlin. West Berlin was an isolated outpost, surrounded by communist East Germany. At the border between West and East, the train stopped, and East German guards wearing great coats and accompanied by German Shepherd dogs came on board, checked our passports and inspected the train. The guards locked the external train doors, keeping us prisoner as we passed into East Germany.

The Accidental Plus One

West Berlin in winter was cold, grey, and bleak. But East Berlin, which tourists were permitted to visit on a day trip, was bleaker still. We arrived at the East German side of the border where guards interviewed my German friend Max while I waited alone in another room.

Later, Max told me how the conversation had gone.

'Your passport has a lot of stamps. Are you a spy?'

'No, I'm not a spy. With a West German passport, you can travel to many places in the world.'

'But it costs money; how does someone your age afford this?'

'By working hard and saving my money. The wages are so much better on the Western side. It doesn't take long to save up for trips.'

The border guard flung Max's passport back at him. Now, it was my turn. But I wasn't worth bothering with as I didn't speak German, and so the petulant officer stamped my passport and sent me on my way. The process had taken over an hour, but at last we were stepping out into the streets of East Berlin.

A condition of the day visa was exchanging a minimum of 25 West German marks for East German ones, equivalent to USD 50 in today's money.

'What do you think they do for coffee here?' I asked Max.

'Instant with chicory, probably.'

'I don't care. We have to spend all this,' I said, proffering the dozens of Eastern Marks we'd had to buy at inflated rates. 'We can't take it back to the West.'

I'd heard other travellers say they ended their day in East Berlin by going to the opera or the theatre, then out to dinner as a way to spend their money. We found a coffee shop, in which we hunkered down as it was snowing. Max talked to a couple of guys our age and translated for me.

He asked them how their lives were. They told him it wasn't too bad; at least they could get Western TV.

This might seem innocuous enough, but these guys were taking a risk by talking to a Westerner. The café, though, wasn't busy and if anyone was listening to their conversation, they didn't seem to care.

I excused myself and nipped to the bathroom. The lock refused to budge when I tried to open the cubicle door. I rattled it, but it was stuck fast. This seemed to go on for ages, but couldn't have been more than five minutes, as I was getting frantic, jiggling the lock and shaking the door.

I looked at my watch. I'd now been gone for ten minutes. And Max wasn't going to come looking for me.

Just my luck the café's quiet. At this rate, I'll be stuck in here until lunchtime. Of all the places to lock myself in a loo, I would pick East Germany.

The door into the women's loos opened, and I heard footsteps.

'Hello, the door is stuck,' I called, thumping the lock.

A reply came back. All I understood was, '*Nyet…*'

Great.

I tried again.

'*Entschuldigung, bitte,*' I pleaded, rattling the door. The woman ignored my feeble German and continued her Russian commentary.

Thanks, lady. Very helpful.

My options were to climb over the top of the cubicle or slide underneath it. I ruled out climbing as the ceiling was so low, I might get stuck. I calculated the gap under the door. It would be tight. I'd put on half a stone since I started travelling, thanks to living on pizza, wine and gelato in Italy. I would have to shed a couple of layers, squeeze my top half out, and then drag the rest of me through, one leg at a time.

The Accidental Plus One

I peered under the cubicle to check first. As the coast was clear, I slid my handbag underneath, but within easy reach in case anyone else walked in. My wallet and passport were in there. I'd need those to get back to the West tonight.

What was I thinking, agreeing to come here?

I'd studied Bertolt Brecht's plays at university and thought we might catch a performance at his famous Berliner Ensemble theatre. But the plan had already fallen over as our timing was wrong. And besides, my admiration for a famous East German playwright wasn't going to get me out of here. I grabbed the clothes I'd taken off and pushed them under the door.

I lay on my stomach and went head first.

Please don't let me get stuck.

It was indeed a tight squeeze, but I eventually managed it, sliding along the cold tiled floor. Thank goodness nobody else could see me—unless, of course, the East Berliners had hidden cameras in their bathrooms. I retrieved my clothes, put them back on, washed my hands, and returned to the restaurant. Max was still at the table, alone, engrossed in a book. He looked up and smiled.

Remind me to choose a more alert travelling companion the next time I go behind the Iron Curtain.

'Everything okay?'

'No, it isn't. If you chat with any other East Berliners, can you ask them if they know the Russian for, "Help, I'm locked in the loo. Please tell my friend Max. He's sitting in the restaurant"?'

'I didn't even notice you'd gone.'

No shit, Sherlock.

'I'll make it up to you. Let's go to the ballet this afternoon, and then tonight, we can eat out. If there's time, we can go to the opera. It finishes at 11, but it still gives us time to get across the border before we turn into pumpkins at midnight.'

'Why not? There's bugger all else to do here.'

East Berlin had not one, but two opera houses. We were going to the Komische Oper or Comic Opera, which was right in the centre, near to Unter den Linden, the Champs-Élysées of Berlin. We saw an elaborate production of *Swan Lake* with a full orchestra for five marks, and when we returned for the opera in the evening, we'd still only spent ten. And even after an evening meal, we had change out of our 25 marks. As we hurried out of the theatre towards Checkpoint Charlie, we discussed what to do about the money we had left.

'Let's give it away,' Max said.

'Are you sure you don't want to buy any last-minute souvenirs?'

'Ha ha. I wouldn't mind a prop from the 1950s hairdresser's.'

'We'd better get rid of it here before the border guards see us.'

Max hurried over to a guy smoking a cigarette in a doorway.

'It's your lucky day, mate,' Max said in German as he handed over all our remaining change. The guy looked up.

'*Danke.*'

'Be funny if he was Stasi,' Max said to me.

'More likely he's clever. We won't be the first to head back across the border at this time of night.'

We stumbled out into the light as we crossed into West Berlin. The streets were awash with neon signs and Christmas decorations. People fell out of crowded restaurants and bars, laughing and chatting, linking arms and heading home. It was buzzing with life despite the bitter cold.

What a contrast to the other side of the border.

Ever since the Berlin Wall came down in 1989, I've vowed to return to see the reunified city in all its glory. When I tell family members where we're going, they ask if they can come too.

Why not? Let's turn it into a family outing.

It's going to be an accidental plus-three jaunt, instead of the usual plus one. We tee up the travel arrangements so we're all on the same flights and staying in the same hotel. On Thursday 28 July 2016, we fly from Heathrow at 19.10, arriving at Berlin-Tegel at 22.00 local time. We take a cab from there to our hotel in Potsdam, arriving at 11pm. It's dark, so we don't get a proper look at the hotel from the outside.

The hotel, it turns out, was built in the late 1960s as part of the Inter chain, meant to lure Western tourists. And it was GDR President Walter Ulbricht who gave the go-ahead to construct the ugly 17-storey edifice, to represent the "socialist crown of the city." Despite it having had a makeover since then, the hotel's older staff are stuck with their 1970s Iron Curtain attitudes.

'Sit there,' the elderly server orders, pointing to a table for four right in the middle of the breakfast area. We ignore her and head for one beside the window with a lake view. She comes running over with a sign saying "*Reserviert.*"

Reserved for who?

'Sit there,' she shouts, insisting we move to the table in the middle.

We give up and do as we're told.

It turns out "sit there" is the only English our waiter

claims to know. Whenever we ask for anything else, she glares at us and says *nein*. First, she needs to take our coffee order.

My sister wants tea.

'*Nein.*'

'Can we have a poached egg rather than a cold hard-boiled one?'

'*Nein.*'

'It reminds me of boarding school,' I say.

'Only with a better view,' my sister replies. True. The restaurant terrace offers sweeping views of the River Havel. Wooden ferry boats ply the river and circuit the lake. It looks idyllic.

'A boat trip would be fun,' I say. But I don't know how we'll fit it in, as we have an action-packed day planned in Berlin.

BB Lookalike bids us farewell as he has to set off for the conference straight after breakfast, leaving the three of us to plan our day. I'm thrilled to have company on one of BB Lookalike's work jaunts, and better still to be accompanied by a German speaker.

The train ride from Potsdam to Berlin Central Station takes half an hour. We transfer to the metro and get on a U-Bahn tube train to the Kurfürstendamm, the ritzy main street in the Charlottenburg neighbourhood. When I was here back in the 1980s, I spent my days walking up and down, marvelling at all the shops. One in particular, the KaDeWe, was then (and still is) Europe's largest department store. It had the biggest and most luxurious food hall I'd ever set foot in, which sold caviar, oysters, eight different varieties of eggs, tropical fruits, exquisite pastries —the epitome of Western decadence when less than a mile away, in East Berlin, I had seen people queuing at butchers' shops for revolting-looking cuts of meat from animals I didn't recognise.

All these years later, the food hall was as I remembered it. We stop for a coffee to linger over the lavish displays of gateaux and tiered cakes, exquisitely iced. I hope to taste some samples, but they don't hand out freebies until we reach the cheese counter. I could spend hours here but must restrain myself as we have lunch plans. Then we head off down the K'damm towards the Hard Rock Cafe, as I'm not the only one going down memory lane on this trip. This one is in a restored Bauhaus building. We go upstairs and sit under some pretty special musical memorabilia, one of which is a guitar said to have belonged to Jimi Hendrix, no less.

After a burger and a local beer (when in Berlin), our final destination on this day out is the Brandenburg Gate. A faded black-and-white photo shows me peering across the Gate at what was once one of the grandest cities in the world, cut into two by an ugly 12-foot high concrete wall. I tried to picture how it might look without it. But my imagination failed me as the bitter wind blew in from the east.

What is a revelation on this trip is how beautiful some of the former East Berlin is and how well the East German elite lived. I believed the propaganda saying everything was better in the West, but I'd only seen one small part of the East, where for most of the population, life was hard.

The most fascinating outing of all is a Red Bus tour, which takes us into an exclusive enclave of Potsdam with lavish houses. Known as Military Station 7, it was a secret walled town where high-ranking Soviet military officers lived and worked. Within the enclave, the former KGB prison stands in stark contrast to the sprawling mansions surrounding it. The building, or what is left of it, is a mass of grey concrete, overgrown and desolate, with tiny slits for windows.

Those poor prisoners. How they must have suffered within these walls.

BB Lookalike has a morning off on Sunday, the day we fly back home, and we make the most of it by walking over the famous Bridge of Spies. In the middle, the halfway point between East and West, prisoners were brought to be exchanged. All the barriers are long gone, but where they stood is still visible.

I'm so grateful I experienced a reunified Germany in my lifetime.

26

Next Stop USA

In late November 2016, I flew out to Perth, Western Australia to join BB Lookalike, who was singing for our supper at a research symposium at Curtin University. We jumped at the opportunity to play tourist for a week over in WA—a much-needed distraction after the Brexit referendum result in June.

We were up in London for a party on the weekend when the results were announced and woke up first thing on the Friday morning to find out how the country had voted. The nightmare scenario became a reality. Too many people had swallowed all the lies and misinformation whipped up by right-wing politicians. Even more shocking, the architects of Brexit forced a rule change so the divisive policy became law by a slim majority, instead of requiring 60 per cent of voters to agree.

We wandered through the capital in a daze, in search of breakfast, meeting bewildered Londoners who struggled to believe the result. This act of economic self-sabotage shocked us both to the core.

BB Lookalike's livelihood depended on European postgraduate students who came to the UK under the Erasmus scheme. With Brexit, they could no longer study here for free, and we had four years to find an exit strategy from Britain so he could stay employed. The trip to Western Australia was no longer solely a pleasant excursion over the British winter; it gave BB Lookalike a chance to find out about future work prospects while we were out there.

On our return from Western Australia, BB Lookalike goes on sabbatical. It's now eight months since the Brexit vote. The government plans to axe Erasmus, even though this decision will affect thousands of British undergraduates, who now won't be able to study in Europe for free. BB Lookalike worries about the inevitable redundancies in higher education after 2020 when the rules come into force.

If you can study in English for free in Sweden or the Netherlands, why would any international student want to pay fees to come to Britain?

Since the Vote Leave campaign won, we've searched for work opportunities in Europe and elsewhere. We both independently qualify for Irish passports, giving us the right to live and work in the EU once Britain leaves. Because he's second-generation Irish, BB Lookalike's right to an Irish passport is automatic. Mine will take longer, as I'm third generation and must become a citizen before I'm eligible. I've started the process, collecting all the birth, death and marriage certificates needed for my application. But the Irish government has been swamped with citizenship enquiries from the six million of us in Britain who have an Irish grandparent. And I'm warned it will take up to six months to process my application.

BB Lookalike receives an offer from Harvard University in February 2017 to be a Visiting Professor for the fall term of the 2017–2018 academic year. A semester in the USA will be another diversion from the Brexit fallout, which has divided not only friends, but families, too.

What prompted the invitation? BB Lookalike thinks it was down to fellow academics working there in the film department. Executive search companies have contacted him in the past about posts at universities in the United States, but so far he hasn't been tempted. The University of California at Berkeley interviewed him a few years back, but he wasn't successful. Once the home of the US counter-culture, the university has now swung in the opposite direction, and his theory is his ideas were too left-leaning for it to countenance.

It was a lucky escape.

Berkeley's house prices are out of our league. We'd have been lucky to afford an apartment. When other Ivy League colleges came calling, we ruled them out as they were on neither the West nor the East Coast.

One matter BB Lookalike must resolve before he can take up the offer from Harvard, is the academic year starts a month earlier in the USA, than in Britain, so his appointment will begin on 1 August 2017 and end on 31 December. He will have to work remotely for the first month as he is teaching in Norway in August.

I make a list of everything we'll need to do to make this happen, starting with our visas. The international office at Harvard sends us information about university-supported work visas and I contact the US embassy in London and book our visa interview appointment. The first available is Monday 26 June at 8.30am. We'll have to take the 5.55am train, arriving at Waterloo at 7.21am, then a hop on the

Jubilee line to Bond Street Tube station. But if the train is late, we risk losing our slot.

We decide to go the night before and stay overnight in a hotel. But on Sunday 25 June, I am taking part in a dressage competition at my riding school. My slot is at 2pm and if I time it right, I can be out of there by four. It's a 30-minute journey home, and I'll need to freshen up.

I pack two bags. One with my dressage outfit (breeches, jacket, stock, and my best riding boots, polished until they gleam). The second bag has London clothes and all the essential paperwork the Embassy requires. I double-check we have everything, including a printed copy of our appointment instruction page and Form DS-160 confirmation. We won't be admitted to the Embassy without them, and it is not possible to print them when we arrive. Old school, then—no flashing your mobile phone with a QR code here. No paperwork, no entry.

My horse Dublin Jack, aka DJ, is on form, and we come third. I bid a hasty thank you to the team and drive home. As it's a Sunday, the traffic is lighter than usual. I make it in 25 minutes and am ready for the London train at 5.30pm. We drive to the station to save time, leaving our car on a side street where there are no parking restrictions. By 7.30pm, we've checked into our hotel in Holborn. By 8pm, we are eating moules-frites at Belgo's, one of the few remaining branches of a favourite chain specialising in Belgian beer and simple but delicious food.

The following day, we're up bright and early, and head out to grab breakfast at the nearest bakery—a branch of Paul, the Belgian chain, where the café au lait and croissants are as good as you'll find in Brussels or Paris. By the time we've eaten, it's 7.30am, and we set off to walk to Grosvenor Square. As far as electronic devices are concerned, we can only bring mobile phones, e-readers, or a tablet. We've left our overnight bags behind at the hotel to collect later, even though they are allowed into the Embassy as they are cabin-baggage size. But they both contain laptops, which aren't permitted.

We get to the Embassy by 7.55am, thinking we're early, only to find the queue snaking across Grosvenor Square.

Everyone else has the same idea.

The line shuffles forward until we reach the entrance, where our belongings are screened and checked. When we enter the building, we're given a ticket number and directed to take the lift to Visa Services on the first floor. We sit in a vast waiting area, bigger than an airport departure lounge, and watch the ticket numbers roll across the screens until it's our turn. Then we are called to a ticket window where we must submit our documents.

The officer at the window glances at our paperwork and asks me what I do.

'I'm a self-employed writer but won't be undertaking any paid work in the United States.'

At least not for any US companies, but why complicate things?

He nods, smiling.

'What do you write?'

'Thriller and memoir.'

'What type of thriller?'

'An environmental one set on five continents—including Antarctica,' I say, passing over my card with my social media handles and the buying links for *Revolution Earth*. He turns the card over.

Wonder if I've made a sale.

Once the documents are submitted, we sit down and wait for our interview, and are instructed to look for the same ticket number on the waiting room screens. Our number flashes up, and we walk towards a separate area where we are called to another window. The embassy official who conducts our interview is a charming woman from New Hampshire, who is keen to know what we will make of Boston.

'Lucky you. It's one of my favourite cities.'

She looks through our documents, stamps them and hands us back BB Lookalike's contract and letter of appointment. 'Your visas will take three to five working days to process. Once they're stamped into your passports, a courier will contact you to arrange a convenient time for delivery. Best of luck, Professor Not Bryan Brown; enjoy your time in Boston.'

It's 10am on Monday morning, and our work here is done. We head back to the hotel to collect our things.

'Wasn't as bad as I thought it might be.'

'It could have been a lot worse,' BB Lookalike says.

I want to skip across Hungerford Bridge towards Waterloo, I'm so excited about our next big adventure. At the station, I buy a guidebook to Boston and read it on the train home.

'US of A, here we come!'

27

The Bostonians

Now we have our visas, the most pressing task is to find a place to live for the fall semester. I'm given the contact details of Harvard University Housing and write to them, but their minimum term is a one-year lease. They can't offer short-term accommodation and send me the link to an off-campus housing site. In short, we're on our own and at the mercy of the private rental sector.

Sabbatical Homes, which lists the houses and apartments of academics and associated staff who are going on sabbatical and need to rent out their properties, pops up on my internet search engine. None of the properties listed will take anything under a six-month lease. And I can't get over how expensive they are for pre-loved family homes with average fixtures, fittings and furnishings.

Based on the prices of the listings, Boston and Cambridge are going to be expensive cities to live and work in. I go on to the comparison website—https://expatistan.com/cost-of-living/comparison/poole/boston. Poole is the closest UK city to Winchester listed, so I compare prices with Boston. It will cost 22% more to live in Boston than in the south of England, because rents are so high.

I sign up with a short-term lettings agency in Winchester to rent out our house while we're away. The garden is awash with spring flowers and the house is looking at its best when the photographer comes to take the photos for their website. It might suit a couple, moving for a new job or renovating their own house. Our village is close to the city, but the tenants will need their own transport as not everyone will want to walk the 1 kilometre to the bus stop or 2 kilometres to the train station.

I am fortunate to have a friend who lives not far from Boston. Over the four months we'll be there, we want to make the most of every single moment, sharing the experience with as many friends and family members who want to visit. And as BB Lookalike will need to work at home in the evenings and at weekends, I alter my search from a one-bedroom to a two-bedroom apartment.

Through Sonder, a private brokering firm, I find the perfect place. It's a two-bedroom/one-bathroom apartment in Cambridge which will cost us US$3,800 a month. We sign up for the property, but a month before we leave, the company contacts us to say the owner is selling up and has withdrawn the apartment. But as we've already signed a lease, Sonder offers us an alternative—a bigger apartment with a second bathroom. The rent, though, will be another $450 a month.

I go online to check it out. It's in Continuum, a brand-new apartment complex in Allston, under a mile's walk to Harvard Square, which is also our nearest subway stop. I do a quick search online for anything else available, but so close to our departure, everything I find is more expensive or further away.

I look at the photos and the layout of the apartment

The Accidental Plus One

again. The entranceway leads into a well-equipped kitchen. To the left, there's a gleaming stainless-steel fridge/freezer, a microwave, a stove, and an oven double the size of the one back home. From what I can see in the photos, there are at least four burners on the gas hob. The splashback has white tiles arranged in a herringbone pattern. The cabinetry is dark brown and there's a kitchen island with two bar stools. Compared with this, my kitchen at home looks tiny.

As we make home-cooked food most nights, I will spend much of my time in this room. It comes with all mod cons with one notable exception—the retro coffee machine. It's a drip coffee maker, a device I haven't seen since my first media job as a lowly receptionist/aspiring copywriter at a *Mad Men* era advertising agency in North Sydney. One of my jobs was keeping two drip coffee makers topped up as the boss drank twelve black coffees daily. He needed them, considering what went on in the boardroom, which you can read about in my memoir *Misadventures in the Screen Trade*.

There's another cultural difference I will have to get used to: despite the cook's kitchen, there's neither a dining table nor chairs.

I don't mind eating breakfast sitting on a bar stool if I'm dining alone, but counters aren't conducive to conversation. Nor do I want to sit and eat dinner on the sofa. A cheap table and four chairs will be the first things I buy as I'm also going to need somewhere to work on my laptop. This is the only glaring omission I can see in an otherwise perfect apartment.

It is spacious too at 1,000 square feet and comes with ample storage space, including a walk-in wardrobe in both queen-sized bedrooms. The living space divides the two bedrooms and their attached bathrooms, so any guests staying will have privacy. The washer/dryer is tucked into a European-style laundry. There's even a cupboard with hanging space for outdoor clothing and shoes in the entrance. We opt to include all linens as part of the agreement so we won't have to bring sheets and towels and get hit with excess luggage charges. In short, we can walk in and start living as soon as we arrive.

There is air conditioning and heating, it's double-glazed (hurrah), and the TV comes with an HDMI cable and a package of international TV channels (which we're going to need). From my experience of television in the United States, there are hundreds of channels, but very few I want to watch. One notable exception is WGBH, the best public television station in the country, which I'm thrilled to note is based in Boston.

The apartment building is secure with a key card needed to get in and a reception with a round-the-clock security guard. Safety—inside and outside the apartment—is crucial as we don't want to be in an area where we are afraid to go out at night. Harvard takes its responsibilities to students and staff seriously. The university has its own police force and call buttons across the campus, which is reassuring, as we intend to walk everywhere we can, and from October onwards it will get dark in the late afternoon. Fortunately, Allston has a high walkability score. When it gets too cold to walk, we plan to rely on public transport and taxis.

The campus has its own subsidised gym with group exercise classes, which I'm intending to sign up to. But our rent at Continuum includes use of its well-equipped onsite gym, which will be handy when the temperatures plummet below zero. It can be as warm as 25–26C in September, so we might spend more time outdoors, but in October, November, and December, we'll be at home most nights.

The Accidental Plus One

We decide to take the Continuum apartment, despite the sky-high rent and the worry about still having to pay the mortgage in Winchester. Nobody wants to rent our place while we're away. Oh well, at least Harvard is covering both our travel expenses.

―

My next task is to find flights to Boston via Oslo, where BB Lookalike is finishing his summer school teaching in August. Luckily, Norwegian not only flies both routes, but has a direct flight back from Boston to Gatwick for our return. Our itinerary will be London Gatwick to Oslo, Oslo to Boston, Boston to London Gatwick. BB Lookalike will fly up to Oslo a week earlier for work and I'll join him for a couple of days before we head to Boston together.

One last requirement we need to fulfil as part of our visa obligations is health insurance. We've never taken out health insurance in the USA and because of our ages, the premium is weighted against us. The most basic cover I can find (excluding dental and major illness) is $400 each per month. And this is after the employer subsidy of $400. As we're away for four months, we'll be unlucky if we need to consult a doctor or a dentist.

'We'd better not get sick while we're away,' I say. 'We can't afford to.'

As we have no takers for our house, I put Plan B in place and pay a housekeeper to come in every couple of weeks to clean and check the place over. I spend my last few days before I leave stuffing as much as possible into my two large suitcases.

On the day of my departure, I allow two hours to get to Gatwick on top of an hour and a half check-in time. My taxi ride is stress free, but I brace myself for the Gatwick experience. It's always crowded and there's nowhere to sit, and today is no different. But the Norwegian check-in and waiting area for Oslo is quiet and free from lager louts, unlike the rest of the airport. And the flight departs right on time.

From the airport in Oslo, I take a cab into the city to our hotel, the Scandic Holberg, 500 metres from the Royal Palace. There are major roadworks right outside our hotel, but the works do stop at night. This is my first visit to Oslo in the summer, so I treat this part of the trip as a mini-break. I've been twice before for work, but it was the depths of winter and I didn't get to do any sightseeing.

BB Lookalike gets back from work at 5pm and we have an early evening drink at one of the local bars, where a mediocre glass of wine costs £15. Luckily, BB Lookalike's colleagues from the University of Oslo have invited me out on the work's dinner and are picking up the tab for that.

We meet at a restaurant a 20-minute walk from our hotel. It's cool for high summer, only 13 degrees, and I'm glad I brought a raincoat and layers. As we're walking back to the hotel after dinner, it's still light. I'm enjoying the long evenings—what a contrast to the Oslo I visited one November, when by mid-afternoon it was dark, and it didn't get light until 9am the next morning.

On Saturday 2 September, the sun comes out. It's turning into a lovely day, the best I've had here so far. But as this is the day we fly, there's only enough time for a quick walk to the art gallery before heading back to the hotel, packing up, and catching a cab at 9am for Oslo-Gardermoen, the airport. We check in for our flight and head off for security screening and border control. There's a holdup because of the distinct lack of staff. Luckily, we've allowed plenty of time, as our flight isn't until 11.50am.

The Accidental Plus One

We land in Boston at 7.20pm, but by the time we make it to the US Customs and Border Protection desk, it's 7.45.

'May I see your passports, please,' the officer says. He's mid-twenties at a guess.

'Our work visas are stamped inside,' I say.

'Sir, may I see your paperwork?'

BB Lookalike opens his laptop to show the officer the digital copies of the rest of the application.

'No, sir, we need printed documents. We do not accept online documentation.'

Ironic the Professor of Film and Digital Media has been told he needs old-school paperwork.

'What if I printed you a copy?' BB Lookalike asks.

'No, sir, I'm sorry.' Before we can say anything, he takes our passports off us.

If this is an episode of Border Force, the officer is going to say, 'Come this way, while we find the next flight to send you home.'

28

Legal Aliens

Look at us, living the American dream. No, wait.

'You need to come with me now,' the young officer says, as he marches us down the corridor.

Bet he's loving this.

He ushers us into a windowless room where every seat is taken and the only available flat space is the floor. We stand.

An elderly couple who don't speak English stare into space; a young father comforts a crying baby; a family with three children want something to eat. What will happen to the Haitian woman and her toddler, talking through an interpreter? We are here as we have all fallen foul of the system—kindred spirits, stuck in this room on a Saturday night, waiting for our names to be called.

Two officials get to decide who can stay and who must go. Imagine what sort of power trip this is for someone as young as the officer who hauled us aside. He plays with his phone between picking up a case file and going through it.

Maybe he's texting his girlfriend. Or watching porn.

Another hour goes by. We told Sonder our arrival time

was 8.30pm. There's no internet and no one can make any phone calls, so there's no way of communicating with the outside world.

A few minutes later, another official, an older woman, sweeps in.

'I want this room processed and emptied by 11pm latest,' she shouts. 'Nobody's going to be sleeping here overnight under my watch.'

Way to go, boss lady!

She grabs half the files from in front of our officer, goes to a separate booth, and calls the first name on the top of the pile.

'Professor Not Bryan Brown?' We jump up and rush over. 'I apologise for holding you up. If this was a weekday in normal working hours, I'd be able to confirm everything with a quick call to the Harvard International Office. But out-of-hours, I can't contact anyone. We operate the same system as the Embassy that processed your application, where we expect printed copies of backup material.'

Oh yes. I remember now. The old DS-160 confirmation page. We wouldn't be admitted to the American Embassy without it and printing it when we arrived would be impossible. Thank goodness for boss lady. She has a brain, even if her idiot younger colleague hasn't.

While we're standing at the counter, listening to the boss, waiting for her decision, her younger colleague lectures an undergraduate student from Poland.

'No,' he says. 'I cannot let you into the United States at this time. I'm sending you back on the next plane. You must go to the Embassy in Warsaw and get the correct visa.' The young woman sighs, her body slumping forward, resigned to her fate. The door opens and an armed uniformed escort leads her away, no doubt to another holding area to wait for the plane.

We may legally enter the country, it says so in our passports.

Okay, we screwed up with the back-up documentation. This student had the wrong visa.

I look up at the clock. It's 10.20pm.

'Professor and Mrs Not Bryan Brown, I can see this is an honest mistake. First thing Monday morning, call the International Office and get them to ring me,' the boss lady says, handing her card to BB Lookalike. 'Welcome to the United States. I hope you have a very pleasant stay here.'

I want to hug her, but I know I can't in case the armed guards think I'm assaulting her. 'Your luggage is being held for you in the arrivals hall,' she calls out after us.

'Thank you,' we say as an officer escorts us out of the detention room and down the corridor.

And sure enough, all our bags are there waiting for us. We load them onto a luggage trolley and make our way across a deserted arrivals area. The glass doors open and we are on American soil.

'Cabs this way,' I say as we walk outside into the fresh air. There's no queue (or line, as I'll need to call it here), so we jump into the first cab.

'Where to?'

'Allston.'

'The traffic's light at this time of night. Should have you folks there in 20 minutes.'

Thank you, boss lady.

'Remember to tip him,' I whisper to BB Lookalike.

'How much?'

'I dunno, 20% of whatever the fare is.'

Another thing we'll need to get used to.

Mercifully, the distance between Logan and Allston is a mere 8 miles, and sure enough, we're there in the promised 20 minutes. While BB Lookalike sorts out the payment and offloads the luggage, I ring the 24-hour bell

The Accidental Plus One

at the side of the building. The concierge comes out to meet us.

'We were held up. I'm sorry.'

'Ma'am, it's okay. I'm here all night. You're in North,' he says, looking at his tablet. 'I need to let you in.' I beckon to BB Lookalike, who is doing his best with all four suitcases.

'Let me help you there, sir,' the concierge says.

'It's very kind of you to offer, but we can manage,' I say, too mean to part with the dollar needed for his help.

We walk down the corridor on the third floor, wheeling our suitcases along the carpet until we are outside our home for the next four months. I push the door open and peer in.

Wow! It's better than in the photos!

Everything gleams and shines. And the crisp white linen in our bedroom tempts, as all I want to do now is crawl into bed.

I sleep through most of the night. The apartment is whisper quiet, with little to no street noise. Our bedroom overlooks a courtyard area, away from the two main roads, and the windows are double-glazed with thick glass. We wake up the next morning at six, make some tea, and head out to the nearest cafe for breakfast, a branch of Swissbakers, right across the street on Western Avenue.

Fortified with an almond croissant and decent coffee, we set off down the road to the nearest supermarket, a Star Market, to stock up and buy supplies for dinner. And as we don't even have salt and pepper, we need to build our pantry from scratch. Checking out a foreign supermarket or food market is one of my favourite past-times, but as we are here for a few months, we aren't window-shopping.

We're limited to what we can carry and buy as many essentials as we can cram into our bags: different types of rice, pasta, spices, oil, butter, eggs, fruit, vegetables. I peer at the frozen seafood section and look at the prices. Jumbo shrimp here is so much cheaper than frozen prawns in the UK. And the Mexican food section occupies an entire aisle, whereas back home, we'd be lucky if it was half a shelf. There are a dozen different brands of corn tortillas in various colours I've never seen before, including purple. And tamale husks, too. Whatever they are, I don't think I'm going to attempt to make them.

I get so distracted by the foreign food section, I nearly forget the coffee filters for the retro machine. The supermarket sells Illy coffee, so I grab a tin.

We have enough ingredients to make jambalaya for this evening—rice, onions, a carrot, celery, tomatoes and shrimp, and fresh coriander. This will do until we've had the chance to check out WholeFoods, where I plan to buy our meat and fresh fish. The nearest store is across the Charles in Cambridge on River Street, a 25-minute walk away. I decide to go there on Monday, when BB Lookalike is due on campus.

It's still early when we get home and unpack our groceries. I'm keen to do a test run with the 1980s coffee machine. As we only need two cups, I halve the coffee in the paper filter and only fill the machine half the way up with water.

The hefty shot of caffeine gives us the energy we need to time the walk to Harvard Square, where BB Lookalike will be based Monday to Friday. It's also the Red Line Metro stop, and all we have to figure out now is how to use the subway so we can take it into Boston.

It's a glorious day and the temperature is forecasted to peak at 27C, so I'm relieved it's still early and isn't too hot yet. We walk along North Harvard Street, a long, straight road which turns into John F Kennedy Street once we cross the Anderson Memorial Bridge. Back in 1915, when the bridge was first built, it carried foot traffic, horses and carts, and those new-fangled cars, the Model T Ford. Today, it's a three-lane highway, but as it's a weekend, the traffic isn't too bad, and we can at least keep up a conversation as we walk across it. To our right on the Cambridge side is the Weald Boat House. It's the size of a large residential house, complete with a pitched roof and two storeys.

As we peer across the bridge, two teams of rowers, one of men, the other of women, sitting backwards in their boats, head towards the bridge, their coxswains' voices bellowing out instructions. There's an identical scene in *The Social Network*, the film about Mark Zuckerberg, the famous Harvard drop-out who left in his second year to create Facebook.

BB Lookalike reckons he can do the journey in 20 minutes if he walks fast, the same time it takes him to get from home to the local railway station.

The metro is a cinch as only one branch line, the Red Line goes to Harvard Square. We buy a ticket, jump on the train heading south, and get off at Downtown Crossing, where we pick up a CharlieCard each at the station, loading them with $50 for the subway. Now it's time to play tourist and make the most of this gorgeous day. We head for the riverfront, starting at the Christopher Columbus Waterfront Park, and plan to walk towards the aquarium.

We haven't gone more than 50 yards before a lilting voice yells at BB Lookalike.

'Hey, Irish, how are yer?' An older man, somewhat dishevelled, comes hobbling towards us. Even though he's after something—money—he has singled out BB Lookalike amongst all the other tourists. Try as I might, I can't stop laughing.

He approaches us, stands a metre away from BB Lookalike, and studies his face.

'It's the nose. Tell you were Irish a mile off.'

Guilty as charged.

Our new friend launches into his life story. An undocumented immigrant from the old country, he tells us, boasting the authorities have yet to catch him. The police turn a blind eye, especially the older guys as they're Irish too. The young ones, not so much now. Maybe he's been lucky. His accent is as unchanged as the day he left, which he tells us was over 30 years ago. I'm not sure where he's from. Kildare? Meath?

We bid him farewell and walk on.

Everyone tells us Boston is full of our people. And they're right.

29

A Very Long Audition

First thing Monday morning, BB Lookalike calls the people in the International Office, who get onto boss lady at immigration. They call us back to let us know the good news: we're legal.

Thank goodness!

We head up to Harvard Square to the nearest branch of Bank of America to open accounts. I notice there is an ATM in Allston, but unlike the one on a street corner in Chicago back in the 1990s I was too scared to use, this one is inside a mini-fortress. And you can only enter the building using a bank card to unlock the door.

I didn't know the expression ATM back then, so was having trouble being understood, as I am now at cafes and restaurants. When I go to order the clear drink from a tap, I get blank stares and a "pardon me, ma'am." I work out I'm making the mistake of putting the letter t in the middle of the word. From now on, I'll say "waaaader" and they'll get it straight away.

Now we're official, BB Lookalike can concentrate on getting his feet under the desk and meeting his students.

His office is in the heart of the Harvard Campus and is next door to the Widener Library, a treasure trove of over 3.5 million books. As the plus one on this jaunt, one of my perks is getting my Harvard Library Reader's Card. I can't wait.

But first up, I need to get through my orientation visit, organised by the International Office. I am the last and only participant because we've arrived one month later than everyone else. My dedicated staff member takes me on a tour of the campus and tells me about all the volunteering and networking I can do while I'm here. There's an organisation called Harvard Neighbours, which is having a Welcome Party on Wednesday 20 September. She will forward the email invitation to me as soon as she receives it.

I am not a joiner and am the least clubbable person I know, so I feel sorry for the lady from the International Office. She's doing her best, though. I don't let on and nod and smile at all her suggestions. All I want out of this session is to get my hands on my library card and find out how to join the gym.

Once the session is over, I meet with BB Lookalike as he has to show his university ID at the library first before I can join. As we stand outside, I glance up.

This is the size of Macy's. I've never set foot in a library this vast before.

Next to this enormous multi-storeyed building, constructed in the beaux arts style, I feel small and insignificant. I linger over the inscription on the plaque in the imposing entranceway: "This library erected in loving memory of Harry Elkins Widener by his mother Eleanor Elkins Widener. Dedicated June 24 1915."

Died 1912. Aged 27. Place of death, Atlantic Ocean.

The Accidental Plus One

Another tragic victim whose life ended on the ill-fated Titanic on her maiden voyage.

From the information I find about Harry, I learn he was a book lover who graduated from Harvard in 1907. As a student, he amassed a collection of over 3,300 volumes. The library is as grand and awe-inspiring as anywhere I have ever been in. Knowing the personal story behind it makes my visit much more meaningful.

As well as the library, I have access to the Harvard gym, which has an Olympic sized swimming pool and runs group fitness classes. I sign up to Zumba, which I've done before, but never with participants from Latin America who really know how to do the steps.

On the Friday at the end of our first week, we go to a faculty party to welcome all the new staff members. It's held at the Carpenter Center. The exterior is brutalist curving grey concrete, the spit of a dreary carpark, but is in fact a building designed by famed architect Le Corbusier.

It hasn't aged well.

I'm introduced to all of BB Lookalike's new colleagues and I forget their names as soon as I hear them. As the wait staff hand out drinks and canapes, I notice a large and boisterous black Labrador among the party-goers who seems intent on hoovering up every dropped crumb.

She's the spit of Zebedee.

Her owners are a German couple here for a year. We swap numbers. When we meet up again, this time at a restaurant, they bring Elsa the Labrador with them. On this evening, she is wearing a harness and a hi-vis jacket with "Service Dog" on it.

I've not seen a service dog run about and chow down on snacks at a party before now.

It turns out she has official status as an emotional support dog. On the plane from Europe, she was even allowed to sit in the cabin! Emotional support animals are in the news in the USA right now, but airline officials are wising up as they have drawn the line at a hopeful passenger who wanted to bring his emotional support peacock to accompany him on a flight.

A few weeks later, BB Lookalike mentions an invitation to an informal lunch with two of his colleagues in the refectory at a student residence. Lunch is in the canteen as promised, where we take our trays up, get given plates and line up at various food stations. I don't think I've eaten this way since living in halls in my first term at university. I'm keen to see the dorm room of Harvard's famous former resident, Mark Zuckerberg. He returned to campus a few weeks back to deliver the commencement address to the class of 2017. It's a shame we missed him.

The couple hosting us make me very welcome and we get a tour of the buildings, during which they stress to us the family atmosphere at Harvard.

And we need to know this because?

As we walk home, I say, 'You know what that was about, don't you?'

'No,' BB Lookalike says.

'An informal interview. They wanted me there to see if I'd fit in to the "Harvard family."There must be a job going. But no one's bothered to tell you yet.'

This seems to come as a surprise to BB Lookalike. 'It's plausible,' he says.

The Accidental Plus One

'Do you want to work here?'

'The students are brilliant, but the office politics…'

'You know when I had the orientation session? I had a feeling there was more to it. I reckon I was being assessed…'

Over the next few weeks, BB Lookalike contacts other colleagues who've either been or are about to teach for a semester.

'What happened to the ones who came here before you?'

'They were sent a letter saying thanks for coming.'

'So, this is a process of elimination until they find the right person. And everything we do here is reported back to the judges and they give us a score out of twelve, as if it's the Eurovision Song Contest.'

'Maybe. I don't know.'

'You'd win the popular vote as your students love you,' I say.

'There's a lot of competition.'

'It's now the jury you have to convince. I wonder if they have a safe candidate lined up as a fall-back.'

This is one hell of a long audition.

───

Meanwhile, back at Continuum, I've been busy making the acquaintance of the various pets in the building. Landlords allowing pets in rental properties is still a novelty for me. What a contrast with Winchester. No one wanted us as tenants because of Zebedee.

The downside to this is there are unsuitable owners in the building with dogs they can't control. An Alaskan Malamute howls from a nearby balcony when it's left outside. I've seen the owner trying to exercise it in the park opposite. It jumps up at people and the young woman lets it happen. I'm sure she loves it, but it's left alone for hours at a time. I blame *Game of Thrones*, the popular hit television series, which made this breed fashionable. They are big, powerful dogs and need a ton of exercise as well as company.

Thankfully, the Malamute lives in the opposite block, as otherwise it would scare the living daylights out of our next-door neighbour, Stella. The first person to make her acquaintance is BB Lookalike.

'Quick. You have to see this,' he says excitedly, running into the apartment.

'See what?' I open the apartment door a couple of inches. 'I don't believe it.'

Trotting down the carpeted corridor is the smallest and pinkest porcine I have ever seen. She barely reaches the height of the skirting board.

'Oink, oink, oink,' she squeaks as she gets closer. She makes a lot of noise for something so tiny and reminds me of a very vocal miniature pony, neighing at the same decibels as a normal-sized horse.

We both get down on the corridor floor. I hold out my finger. She bites it with her blunt little teeth. I want to pick her up and cuddle her, but it isn't fair, as she doesn't know me. Instead, I marvel at the size of her tiny hooves.

Now we have met Stella the micro-pig, known on the rental agreement as a "small dog," we keep her a secret. Every evening, I open the door to see if she is out playing in the corridor. But every evening other than the first one, I'm disappointed.

If I stop pestering her owners every time I see them about how Stella is doing, maybe she'll show up?

The next time I catch up with Mr and Mrs Stella is after Thanksgiving. I'm sure they've been avoiding me.

The Accidental Plus One

They went to Connecticut for the holiday weekend, they tell me, and Stella hated the car journey in her cat crate.

Fur kids, eh? Only in America.

But then, this is also the America where the current president is a billionaire and former reality TV host. A cult figure who bragged about his wealth, persuaded ordinary people he had their interests at heart. Within the bubble of two of the world's leading universities, there won't be many here who admit to voting for him. On the east coast, from Maine to Maryland, is a blue wall. However, this vast country is polarised, and many people living in the rural heartlands, who feel neglected, have very different opinions.

It turns out I don't have to wait long to hear what the ordinary folk here think of him. As soon as they hear my accent, they give their opinions.

'You're from England? Whaddya want to come here for? We have Trump!' says the lady running the dining car on the train between Boston and Washington DC. I can tell by her accent she's a New Yorker. From Brooklyn, to be precise. 'Sure as hell, I didn't vote for him. Now, what can I get you folks?'

Because of our run-in with US Immigration at the border, we are terrified of leaving the country between now and the end of December. But we need to find somewhere warmer than here to go to over Christmas week, when the university shuts down and Boston will be miserable. In England, people complain it's freezing when the temperature drops to zero. Here, the temperature drops to minus 26C and it's too cold to wait at a bus stop as your eyelids are in danger of freezing over. Yet the construction workers still have to work outdoors in these conditions.

Our only two options, where it's guaranteed to be warm in December, are Hawaii or Florida. Hawaii is 11 hours by plane from Boston and expensive for a Christmas break. Boston to Miami is 3 hours 30, with flights and accommodation half the cost of travelling to Hawaii.

We focus on the latter option and choose Florida, as it will be the warmest place in the country. The other attraction is there are no freshwater estuaries, where we're going, which means fewer alligators, although this doesn't deter the American crocodile. Still, there's one major problem. In September, Hurricane Irma, a Category 4 with wind speeds of 130mph (210km/h), wiped out much of the infrastructure. And Cudjoe Key took a direct hit. There are so many heartbreaking stories of people who lost their homes and livelihoods and have to live in temporary housing; the last thing they need are tourists over Christmas.

I wait until late November to book. Then I watch a news report stating the Keys are reopening for business. Not all facilities will be open for Christmas, and some beaches will have limited access, but the hospitality industry needs tourists, the report concludes. We'd rather spend our tourist dollars where they're needed, so we decide to go.

I've only ever been to Florida for work in Orlando. And all I know about the Keys are they were a magnet for artists and writers and their most famous resident was Ernest Hemingway, who lived in Key West. On this trip, his house is a must-visit, but because we aren't hiring a car, we'll need somewhere central in the Keys to stay. I pick Marathon, halfway between Miami and Key West. What swung it is it's the base for Aquaventures Eco Tours, a kayak company which takes you out to spot manatees.

All we need now is a hotel.

Out of the 20 hotels in the area, only a handful have reopened after the hurricane. One stands out, the Courtyard by Marriott Faro Blanco Resort. We book ten days at the hotel.

'We're going to have to mind our Ps and Qs in Florida,' I say. 'They love Trump down there.'

BB Lookalike shakes his head. I hope we can avoid politics on holiday.

30

Driving Miss Bree

As it's been years since I've driven on the "wrong" side of the road and never in the USA, I use the opportunity while I'm here to get a driving lesson, in case we need to hire a car at Christmas. But all the driving schools are ridiculously expensive, and they expect you to sign up for a half dozen lessons, when all I need is one.

A small owner-operated school is much cheaper than all the others.

How bad can it be?

I phone the owner and we meet the following day outside the apartment block. A short and muscular man in his sixties pulls up in a scruffy car. He rolls down the window and greets me in Eastern European-accented English.

'Hello, I'm Igor.' He exits the driver's seat and tells me to get in. I do as I'm told. I will drive us on the suburban streets of Boston, and then on the highway. There's no arguing. But this car is automatic and my car in England isn't.

I run through my usual spiel in my head: my right foot

operates the brake and the accelerator. The left one taps along to the music. I play the Bee Gees *Stayin' Alive* in my head and tap along, taking Igor by surprise.

'What are you doing?'

'Tapping my left foot. My car back home is a manual.'

'Stick shift. If Americans had to drive those things, I'd have no work. Americans, some of them are stupid,' Igor says. 'You Europeans, you are clever.'

I hope I live up to his expectations.

'You're not fond of America?'

'No, I love America. Been here 30 years. I love America so much, I'm showing you my American house.'

Despite all the street furniture and confusing signage at intersections—or cross streets, as they call them here—I spot we are in Brighton and driving in a very smart neighbourhood.

'There, the grey one,' Igor says. My eyes are on stalks when they should be on the road. It's huge but tasteful with white shutters. A house straight out of *Desperate Housewives*. Yet here we are in a dirty, beat-up car.

How can Igor afford a mansion on a driving instructor's income? Something doesn't add up. How does he make his money? Arms dealer? Human trafficker?

Stop making up stories about him and keep your eyes on the road.

'And have you been back home since you left?' I say, which is my way of finding out which Eastern European country he's from. He falls for it.

'Russia? A few times.' He doesn't elaborate.

He shut down that conversation.

At the end of my lesson, we've driven all over Boston suburbia and on the freeway. I'm getting the hang of it.

'Shall I drive back to Allston now?'

'No, the next pupil drives the last one home. Those are the rules. Pull up here.'

The next pupil? No way, pal. I'm not having a learner drive me home.

'It's fine, Igor. I'll get out here and make my way home.'

'No, you get in the back of the car!' he shouts. I want to tell him where to go, but his tone is menacing and I came out with no money, apart from the $50 I gave him for the lesson. As any sane person might assume, I thought he'd drop me off outside my apartment and not force me to go on a white-knuckle ride with a learner driver. Is it even legal? I don't dare write a scathing review on Google, in case Igor comes after me.

This is why he has glowing reviews on his website. His pupils are terrified of him.

I slump down on the back seat as a nervous teenager gets in, while Igor lights a cigarette. I want to flee, but don't want to leave this young girl alone with Igor either. If she's going to be driving me, I need to give her some reassurance.

'Hi, I'm Alison. You been driving long?'

'I'm Bree. This is the first time I've ever driven. I'm scared.'

Oh great. This is how it ends.

I want to get out of the car, but with no money and clueless about where I am, I stay put. I can't call BB Lookalike as he's at work and he wouldn't know how to find me anyway, so I will give this kid all the encouragement she needs to get me home.

Igor gets in the car and tells Bree to start the engine. And then we're off. Bree drives slowly, but impatient drivers behind her honk their horns.

'Go faster,' shouts Igor.

Stop bullying her!

Bree approaches the traffic lights at a big intersection.

If she doesn't connect with the brake, then we're toast. Ignoring Igor's shouting, she pulls to a stop.

'You're doing great, Bree,' I say as I look out the car window and see we are only a mile from Allston. 'I have to go to the library,' I lie, 'so you can drop me here.' Before Igor has time to interrupt, Bree pulls over and comes to a halting stop. 'Best of luck, Bree,' I call over my shoulder as I make my escape.

No, I don't need another lesson, thanks, Igor.

31

Manatees and Mangroves

It's 18 December and minus 1C at Logan. Snow blankets the tarmac, and the plane needs a thorough de-icing before we can take off. I can't think of a better day to get out of here. From my window seat, I peer down at the snow-covered ground below as we fly south. It's only once we reach Virginia the snow disappears.

In Miami, it's 29C, and a driver is waiting to take us to Marathon. Our timing is bad as we've hit rush hour. Getting out of the arrivals area takes long enough. People here drive with the same aggression as those in Rome, with cars beeping their horns and coming at us on all sides. I'm so thankful it's not me behind the wheel.

We crawl through the traffic until we reach the main road south, the I1 or Overseas Highway. There isn't much of a view from the four-lane highway, but we catch glimpses of the water every now and again. The further south we drive, the more evidence there is of the terrible toll from Hurricane Irma. We see houses with roofs torn off, as well as fences and front yards destroyed. And beside the highway are fridges, washing machines, sofas and furniture piled high, all ruined.

We arrive at the hotel two and a half hours later at 7pm. For once, the reality lives up to the photos. At 7.30pm, we're sipping evening drinks and dining on coconut shrimp.

The next morning, after breakfast in the hotel dining room, run by charming Spanish-speaking staff, we are ready to get out and explore on foot. This is, of course, not normal in a place where everyone drives, and the only footpath is the sidewalk along the four-lane highway. Our destination is a wildlife centre, two miles along the road. The route passes the shopping area, where we spy shops selling swimming and surfing gear, most of which have sales. I find a long-sleeved sun-proof top to wear over my swimmers, as well as deck shoes. BB Lookalike opts for two dubious-looking polyester tropical shirts.

Betty and Marty are the two staff members on duty at the wildlife centre. Betty is a busy retiree in her late 70s.

'How did you cope here at the centre in the hurricane?' I ask as she sells us our tickets.

'Trees came down. We're still cleaning up. Marty's been doing that today.'

'And at home?' Betty looks up from the desk, her pale blue eyes welling up with tears. She pulls out a tissue from her pocket and blows her nose.

'We were told to evacuate, and I put the cat in her cage and drove for 11 hours to my daughter's in Georgia. It was one helluva drive. There were so many cars on the highway.'

'I'm so sorry. How is it since you came back?'

'Not so good. I no longer have a home and I'm living in a trailer park.' Betty reminds me of Mum, and if I were her daughter, the last thing I'd want is for her to be living in a mobile home.

Before I have a chance to say anything to comfort her, she lets rip.

'And as for Trump, he hasn't even set foot in the Keys, even though it took a direct hit.' BB Lookalike and I look at each other. 'I've voted Republican all my life. But this man is a disgrace to the memory of Abraham Lincoln.'

'We're so sorry, Betty. Are you getting any government help?'

She shakes her head. 'Not yet.'

'But you're still working here despite everything.'

'It gets me out of the trailer park.' She pauses, collecting her thoughts. 'Thank you, folks, for coming here. We need you. And here's Marty,' she says.

It's Marty who will take us on the tour.

'You folks will have heard of our 45th President?' We nod, which is our way of encouraging him to say more. 'I was called up and served in Vietnam, along with all my comrades. I didn't have a rich father who persuaded a doctor to concoct a medical exemption. What was it for now? Bone spurs!'

These stories have a profound effect on me. We didn't intend to come here to talk politics. But Betty and Marty represent a sector of society which the current administration doesn't care about. Why have your picture taken with two older American volunteers who lost their homes in Hurricane Irma, when you can have a photo-op with a dictator from North Korea?

We take the direct bus from Marathon to Key West on 26 December, which isn't a public holiday in America. It's a

The Accidental Plus One

49-mile round trip. When BB Lookalike gets on the bus, the young driver takes one look at him and charges him two dollars, the seniors' rate for a return ticket. He doesn't even bother to check his ID.

This has to be the bargain of the century.

'Make it two,' I say, keeping my sunglasses on.

'Four dollars,' the driver says without looking up. I suppose I should feel indignant he thinks I look old enough to be a senior, but the cost savings are too good to bother. Florida's retired community is awash with facelifts, fillers, and Botox, so I guess it's very hard to tell someone's age.

Not only is the bus trip the bargain of the century, but this journey takes in the most scenic part of the Keys. After Marathon, we cross the Seven Mile Bridge, an important route linking the Middle Keys to the Lower Keys. We are on the modern concrete one, but look out towards the old bridge, built in the early 1900s for the railway. It's amazing it's still standing, given the hammering it must have received by Hurricane Irma.

It takes an hour to get to Key West. As we enter the city, the vegetation is looking tropical. We get off the bus amongst a sea of people, all wearing lanyards of various colours. To get our bearings and admire the scenery, we walk out towards the waterfront, but right in front of us, blocking the view, is a nine-storey edifice, the cruise ship *Costa Deliziosa*. And then I spot not one, but two other giant cruise ships.

No wonder the place is heaving.

If each ship carries 3,000 passengers, they must increase Key West's population (26,000) by a third. There will be a lot of competition to find somewhere for lunch.

As it's still only 11am, we grab a coffee at a lively restaurant on the main street. Across the road is a poster for an art exhibition of the original illustrations of John J Audubon's *Birds of America*.

'It's the world's most expensive book,' BB Lookalike tells me.

'How expensive?'

'Millions in today's money.'

'Fascinating. Let's go,' I say.

It is one of the most staggering exhibitions I have ever been to. We have unfettered access to every single illustration, as there are only eight other visitors at the gallery. I think of the hordes of cruise ship passengers and am thankful none of them know about this. Each exhibit is a masterpiece of botanical painting.

'The last copy of the book in private hands sold for $8,802,500 in 2000,' the curator tells me.

How lucky are we to get to see this?

'Let's brave the Hemingway House,' I say as we leave.

Sure enough, as we approach, there is a long line of visitors wearing coloured lanyards waiting to get in. But their tour group leader decides the line is too long and walks away. The coloured lanyards do the same. And we're now at the head of the line.

The house is a sprawling two-storey building in the Spanish Colonial style, dating from 1851. Second wife Pauline's uncle bought it for the Hemingways in 1931 as a generous present for the couple. The house needed extensive work to make it into a home, which the Hemingways undertook in the early 1930s. In 1937, work began on the in-ground swimming pool, which is said to have cost a staggering $20,000. It was the first and only one of its kind for 100 miles.

Hemingway's studio is in a separate building, up some stairs. It's my perfect writer's room, with a desk, office chair, and armchair for reading. I'm not sure I'd do much work up here as the outlook is so beguiling, I'd end up staring at the swimming pool and the tropical garden.

The author lived in the Key West house with Pauline for nine years, but after their divorce in 1940, he moved to Cuba with Martha Gellhorn, his third wife. Hemingway was a product of his time and although I'm not a fan of his behaviour, I admire his writing and dedication to his craft. I can believe he rewrote the opening to *A Farewell to Arms* over 50 times. It must have helped that the Hemingways had a team of invisible staff who took care of all the mundane chores—caring for children, cooking and running a household—thanks to Pauline's rich uncle supplementing their income.

A visit to this house seems the perfect way to end our Christmas escape from the Harvard Bubble. We say goodbye to Florida and head back to Boston, but our plane from Miami goes via Newark in New Jersey. When I explain to our fellow passengers we have a tight connection to make our Boston flight, we are met with gum-chewing indifference.

'Too bad, lady, we all gotta be somewhere.'

Imagine being in an emergency landing with this lot. They'd still be fishing their luggage out of the overheads, not letting anyone through when the plane went up!

We make a run for it as soon as we are off our plane and get our connecting flight, despite our fellow passengers doing their best to block our way. On arrival in Boston, we have only four days left until our visas run out at midnight on New Year's Eve 2017. And we have a lot of packing to do before we catch our 8.20pm flight back to the UK on 31 December. One of our jobs is to re-home all the additional furniture we bought here, including the cheap table and chairs. Luckily, several charities in Cambridge do this. I phone Furnishing Hope of Massachusetts, which helps homeless families move into their own home. They are happy to take anything I can donate. I call a cab, load up and drop everything off.

At Trader Joe's on the ground floor of our building, we bump into Stella's mum and dad. As they cook at home, we offer them all our herbs and spices, and they say yes. Later that day, we knock on their door. As a thank you, they invite us in and offer us a glass of wine.

My last chance to play with the pig.

Over in the corner of the living room is Stella, playing on her own in a doggy pen. She even has a litter tray in there. The Greta Garbo of pigs, Stella wants to be alone and turns her back on me, playing hard to get. I give up and chat with our hosts.

We leave Boston as scheduled on New Year's Eve. Our seat companion, a junior business executive, is travelling to work with the most shocking cold. He must have a high fever, as he's shivering. By rights, he shouldn't be travelling at all. I feel sorry for him, but wish he wasn't sitting next to us, as I'm convinced we will catch his bugs.

By the time we arrive at Gatwick, it's 2018.

Some months pass before BB Lookalike hears from Harvard. The correspondence is full of praise for his contribution to the department during the fall term. But we find out through the grapevine the university did as predicted and appointed the safe candidate for the job.

32

Not Quite Noma

While Boston might have solved our immediate problem of where to earn a living post-Brexit, we're glad our future won't be in the USA. We'd prefer to stay in Europe, but nothing has come up so far.

Still, plenty of short-term opportunities come our way, and at the end of May 2018, we fly from London Heathrow to Copenhagen, arriving at 5.30pm. The metro train taking us into town is full as it's rush hour. A guy, mid-twenties and in a suit, pulls his tie down to loosen it. A businesswoman undoes the top button of her shirt.

So it's not only me. Is the heating on?

I go for it and take my jacket off, hooking it over my arm.

'This can't be normal,' I say to no one in particular. Checking the weather app on my phone, I do a double take. There's a lot of cool things in Denmark, but today, the weather isn't one of them. It's 28C. And no, I haven't made a mistake and pulled up the forecast for Casablanca rather than Copenhagen.

I own two Danish-designed raincoats, so I figured it

must rain a lot here. I'm now regretting having packed too many warm clothes, although I did bring a few t-shirts.

We get out at Nørreport Station as advised by our hosts and spend the next ten minutes dragging our suitcases towards Vester Voldgade. It's a busy street and I don't expect Hotel Kong Frederik will be quiet. But we've been assured the rooms booked for conference delegates face away from the road.

I look up at the hotel building. It's white with at least six floors and, by the looks of the ornate balconies and window decorations, late 19th century. We walk into a stylish reception area with charcoal grey carpets and walls, papal purple touches, and inviting mustard yellow sofas. While BB Lookalike shows the receptionist his conference booking, I spot the wall plaques. They're a roll call of celebrities who have stayed here, from Archbishop Desmond Tutu, to Duran Duran, to Diana Dors. I've seen the Archbishop dressed up in a bright purple outfit as though he was Prince's godfather, so I bet he loved the décor. And as for Diana Dors, I reckon it suited her too.

I look over towards check-in, where the receptionist is handing over free earplugs and a large old-fashioned key to BB Lookalike.

'Yes to the earplugs,' I say.

The receptionist's knowing smile says, 'You're going to need them' as she directs us to what is the top floor. The lift is a typical European one and a tight squeeze with the two of us and our suitcases. On the top floor, the heat hits us with full force. And there appears to be no ventilation as we walk along the creaking corridor.

We unlock the door to our room, a cosy attic. I peer in.
Remind me to come back in the middle of winter.

We fling open the tiny windows as wide as they'll go, all of six inches. The conference organisers have been as good as their word. The room looks out to a side street. The view is over the Town Hall Square, which is adorned with a large clock tower that chimes seven times.

'It's 7pm. And still boiling. I'm going to see if they can give us a fan, as otherwise we'll cook,' I say, dumping my bag and belting downstairs to reception. Luckily, the receptionist takes pity on me and room service arrives ten minutes later with an antiquated but working fan.

We might even sleep.

'Shall we eat here this evening? The restaurant is Italian,' I say.

'Let's go down and drink in the bar, and then decide.'

We scan the menu, which offers authentic Italian pizza with thin crusts and traditional toppings, and pick a street table as the temperature is still in the high twenties. I order a white pizza with rosemary, Taleggio cheese and potato. But even though it's carb on carb, the potato slices are so thin, they're see-through. And it tastes delicious.

We walk through the town centre to get our bearings and have a nightcap after dinner, and then head back to the hotel. When we return to our room, we crank the fan up to full throttle and open the tiny attic windows again. As we're in the middle of the city on a hot night, all the street noise drifts in, despite us being on the top floor. I lie in bed, wide awake, and hear the chimes from the clock tower in Town Hall Square strike every hour.

Oh please, say this isn't going to go on all night.

I don't need to look at my watch when the chimes ring out twelve times.

Clocks often feature in Hans Christian Anderson's stories. This thing must have kept him awake.

Hans Christian Anderson, I find out later, spent twenty years in Nyhavn, fewer than two kilometres from Town Hall Square. Even if it is a bit of a stretch to think the author heard the chimes, back in the 19th century there was less street noise. While trams and horse-drawn carriages must have made a racket, there wasn't the constant din of traffic or the screams and yells from the funfair at Tivoli Gardens.

With my earplugs in, I nod off and sleep without waking for six hours. Mercifully, the clock doesn't strike up again until 8am.

After breakfast in the hotel, BB Lookalike gets prepped for the paper he is giving at the seminar at SMK, the National Gallery of Denmark. I'm planning to wander along the canals, soak up the history of the place and gawp at a few shops. My first stop is Christiansborg Palace, a kilometre away from our hotel, to visit the ceremonial horses owned by the Danish Royal Family. As it will be another 28C day, I decide to do all my walking in the morning before it gets too hot.

The entrance fee is 65 kroner—a bargain £7.50—to see the Royal horses. Christiansborg Palace is still a royal residence, so the place shuts to the public when Queen Margrethe is in residence. But not today. I time my visit to see the horses being schooled in the riding grounds in front of the palace. It's a treat to watch these magnificent animals strutting their stuff.

The 20 horses kept at the palace come from two distinct breeds. The Kladrubers, from the Czech Republic, are one of the oldest horse breeds in the world, and Danish Warmbloods are a type of sports horse. In the palace's heyday (no pun intended) at the end of the 17th century, horse lover King Christian V kept 170 of the animals with over 150 staff to look after them. There have been horses

The Accidental Plus One

in the royal stables since the year 1590. In June, they will be moved to their summer pastures in North Zealand, so I'm very fortunate to get to see them.

Above the royal stables is another must-see on my day's itinerary, the Theatre Museum in the Court Theatre, a collection dating from the 18th century. As well as looking at displays of costumes, props and set designs, I wander through the theatre itself. It's a lovely, intimate space and I'd love to see a performance here. Perhaps next time.

I spend the rest of the day wandering past the canals, as well as taking a boat trip. This takes in Freetown Christiania, an abandoned former military base still known as the anarchists' go-to neighbourhood. A group of hippies squatted in Christiania in 1971 and cannabis has been freely traded for fifty years. Today, 900 people live in what is an autonomous community independent of the Danish state, with its own rules and regulations.

But the site the tourists all want to see is not the hippy commune, but the very spot where convicted murderer Peter Madsen moored his homemade submarine, UC3 *Nautilus*. Ten months ago, Madsen lured Swedish journalist Kim Wall out onto the sub, promising her a story. Instead, he abused and murdered her in a case which gripped the world's media.

Madsen's case is still fresh in everyone's minds as it is only a month since his conviction and sentence. Kim was 30 and had most of her life in front of her before Madsen cut it so brutally short. She'd already achieved so much in her career, only to be killed doing the job she loved.

I try not to dwell on what happened to Kim as I wend my way back to the hotel at 5pm to get ready for tonight's seminar dinner, which the organisers have invited me to. I'm looking forward to it as Copenhagen has a groundbreaking restaurant scene. René Redzepi, the chef-patron of Noma, is a global superstar credited with inventing New Nordic Cuisine. The booking is for 7pm at Restaurant Kaptajn, which is rumoured to be run by one of his protégés. We are going to be served a ten-course tasting menu. BB Lookalike and I have adventurous tastes and eat most things, so have chosen the omnivorous option.

After his nonstop day at the conference, BB Lookalike meets me at the hotel, and we set off to walk to the restaurant, twenty minutes away. It's a pleasant stroll through a park to the trendy part of town between Nørrebro and Østerbro. The venue is in an old warehouse, and the view is of Sortedam Dossering, a street running along the western shore of Sortedam Lake.

Twenty of us sit at one large table and as we start the introductions, the first of the ten courses arrives. According to the server, it is a homemade bread roll with signature seaweed butter. The staff seem quite amateurish, plonking the food on the table. Fortunately, the sommelier, who offers us a wine match for each course, knows his stuff. We clink glasses and drink a toast.

'*Skal*!'

While we are making small-talk, the front of house staff bring us the second course. As I take another sip of wine, I look at my plate in horror. It might be prettily dressed with micro herbs, but there's no escaping I'm about to eat raw meat—steak tartare. I eat with my eyes first and I've always thought the presentation is lacking in the way this dish is served, so I've never ordered it.

I dig in. At least it's well seasoned and I eat most of it.

I ask my immediate neighbours at the table if they know how famous the Copenhagen restaurant scene has become, and they shake their heads and laugh.

'We are not used to this kind of food,' one of them says.

'What do you eat at home, then?'

'Pork is popular, served with potatoes. Or baked fish, meatloaf. Plain food.'

No wonder they're bemused by this restaurant.

The second course is a salad of lamb's lettuce and dried shaved truffle. Then comes a house-made cheese in a butter emulsion sauce and fresh chervil. Course number four is a pan-fried dourade (fish) with shavings of fresh beetroot, shallot and samphire in a sauce made from foraged mushrooms. This is my favourite course so far. It's followed by a lemon sorbet.

By course number six, which is pork, but not cooked in a way anyone here recognises, the waiting staff are short-tempered. They no longer give us descriptions of the dishes as they slap the food on the table. Course number seven is another palate cleanser and course number eight, an assortment of cheeses. Nine is dessert and ten is coffee with petit fours and the bill. The entremets are served on a white two-tiered plate, so at least there is someone left in this restaurant who is still trying. I choose a mini lemon meringue pie, a square of chocolate with salted caramel on top, plus a strawberry truffle. They're all delicious.

I don't know how much the bill comes to, but with wine matches and ten courses, it must have been a lot. By the looks on the faces of BB Lookalike's colleagues, I doubt if any of them will want to eat here again.

Postscript

According to its Facebook page, in May 2020, the restaurant had to close due to the impact of the COVID lockdown.

Being big fans of Scandi-noir, we decide to do some set-jetting and go on *The Bridge* tour on BB Lookalike's day off. Spending a day crisscrossing the Øresund Bridge might seem strange if you've never seen the series and don't know what the fuss is about. It follows two cops, one Swedish and one Danish, who join forces to investigate not one but two murders after bodies are found in the middle of the bridge on the border between their countries. Because of the innovative script and outstanding performances by the ensemble cast, the series has a cult following.

When we line up in Copenhagen for the bus connecting Denmark and Sweden, we find out we aren't the only people who've thought to do this. Marjorie and Helen, two pushy Australian ladies in their 80s, are standing in line, ready to board in front of us. They make a beeline for the front seats.

'It's the best view,' Marjorie calls out.

Yes, we noticed. Anyway, all the advice I've read online is you get a better one on the way back from the Swedish side.

As they know they've beaten us to the best seats, they swivel round to chat with us.

'We came all the way from Sydney to do this,' Helen says.

'We're widows, you know,' Marjorie adds. 'And we love *The Bridge* and all the other Scandinavian crime series; the scarier, the better.'

'We watch them together as otherwise we wouldn't be able to sleep at night.'

'Where do you live in Sydney?' I ask, guessing by their elegant jewellery it's in the swish Eastern Suburbs.

'Double Bay,' Marjorie says.

Ha ha. Knew it!

'We've been on cruises together, and when we're home,

we even go to the,' she lowers her voice, "beautician" together.'

Helen laughs, embarrassed. 'You're giving away all our secrets, Marj.'

'I don't care,' Marjorie says, patting her face. 'You can't tell I've had work, can you?'

'Not at all,' I lie.

All of a sudden, they abandon the chat and grab their phones.

'Cameras ready, here we go. Look down there, Helen. It's where Saga and Martin found the bodies, I'm sure of it.'

I peer down, but hold off on my photography for the return journey.

'Ladies and gentlemen,' the Danish bus driver announces, 'we are now approaching the Swedish border, where we will stop and Swedish immigration will board the bus and ask to see your passports. Make sure you have all your identity documents ready. They are much stricter on the Swedish side than we are in Denmark.'

This sounds like the sibling rivalry between Australia and New Zealand.

The bus comes to a stop, and we wait five minutes. A bored-looking Swedish immigration officer doesn't even bother to get on board and waves us through the checkpoint.

We spend the day strolling through Malmö, walking along the foreshore, buying a sandwich and a drink, and enjoying an impromptu picnic in the sunshine. On the return bus trip, we get to the bus station early and are first in the queue. I look for Marjorie and Helen, but they're nowhere to be seen. Once the driver arrives, we nab the best seats in the house and prepare for our photoshoot.

I hum the theme tune, *Hollow Talk*, in my head as we

approach the bridge. My version is not a patch on the real thing by The Choir of Young Believers, but it gets me in the mood for the drama of the view as I look out my window. The Øresund Strait, connecting the Baltic with the North Sea, shimmers in the afternoon sunshine. It's too lovely a day for the discovery of two bodies in a grisly double murder.

While the theme of the first season was about connecting the two countries and encouraging freedom of movement, by the second, the bridge had become a way of keeping borders secure and people out. And it's mirrored by the way we are greeted on our return from Sweden at the Danish border. The Danish immigration officer comes on board the bus and asks to see our passports and identity cards.

We don't see Marjorie and Helen again. But long may they enjoy their adventures together and who knows, we might catch up with them on another set-jetting jaunt sometime soon!

33

Melbourne Calling (Again)

In 2019, BB Lookalike gets an email from an ex-colleague at the University of Melbourne, sounding him out for a job vacancy coming up, this time in a smaller department than the one he ran before. It's my fault. I opened my big mouth after visiting for a family wedding.

'I'd be willing to give the place another go. Only this time, we'd do it differently and live on the southeast side, not the west. St Kilda, maybe?'

I give my blessing, knowing deep down he's going to get the job. I rationalise this move by saying I'll do it, provided I can come back to what is supposed to be our forever home every summer.

And on New Year's Eve 2019, we set off for Heathrow.
Here we go again.
But I'll save that story for another day.

Postscript

"Trailing spouse" wasn't an option in the careers course I attended while in school back in New Zealand all those years ago. If it had been, the young me would have been the first to scoff at it. But it's what I've been, on and off, for the past 20 years.

In 1981, journalist Mary Bralove coined the phrase in the *Wall Street Journal*, in a piece about executive recruitment. When one partner in a relationship is offered a job and asked to relocate, often it's a struggle for their other half to find work. Suppose they can't find a suitable position, or are prevented from seeking employment in an overseas relocation because of visa issues? Then they are referred to as the trailing spouse, a brutal label to give anyone, especially someone about to make a major lifestyle change.

Other trailing spouses include Hillary Clinton and Michelle Obama, who put their legal careers on hold to move to the White House. Doug Emhoff (married to US Vice President Kamala Harris), moved to Number One Observatory Circle, Washington DC. Julia Child went to live in France when her husband Paul, who worked for the US State Department, was posted there in the late 1940s, and while there, reinvented herself as a cook.

It is certainly not a flattering description for someone who may have once been the higher earner in the relationship, but as I was the instigator of one of our major lifestyle changes, I have no one to blame but myself. And while I may have had to forge a new identity, I already had a support network of family and friends for many of our moves.

There are kinder ways to describe my tribe, such as accompanying spouse or expat partner. I refer to myself as the accidental plus one. If I could go back in time and tell the young, arrogant youthful me this is how her life would pan out, she'd laugh in my face. But upping sticks and criss-crossing the globe has had its moments. And I wouldn't have exchanged this life for any other or all the money in the world.

Author Note

Thanks so much for reading this book. If you enjoyed it, I would love it if you would leave a review on your favourite book review website. It doesn't have to be a long one. Even a line or two makes all the difference.

Acknowledgments

I am so grateful to Alison Jack for her meticulous and generous developmental and copy editing. Once again, I am very fortunate to have the input of beta reader Stephanie Light, who read the manuscript not once but twice and saved me from making many embarrassing mistakes.

Thanks once again to Andrew Brown of Design for Writers for his imaginative book cover, which perfectly captures the tone of this memoir.

And most of all, my heartfelt thanks go to Not Bryan Brown for all his hard graft at the day job, without which I'd never be able to write full-time.

About the Author

Alison Ripley Cubitt started her writing career at age nine by winning first prize in a writing competition with a pony book. Some years later, she left New Zealand with the ability to make a white sauce without a recipe, carry three plates at once, and ride a horse (though not at the same time). Dreaming of becoming a copywriter, she landed a job as the receptionist in an advertising agency in Sydney that made the TV series Mad Men's work culture look tame.

But the lure of London proved too hard to resist, and she left Australia. Landing in London at the right time, she got her break in television production and lasted 15 years, working on Channel 4's anarchic The Big Breakfast and at Walt Disney and the BBC.

For the past four years, she has divided her time between Melbourne, Australia and Jane Austen country, England.

An accomplished author of non-fiction works, including two travel guides and three memoirs, her literary achievements encompass works of fiction, from screenplays to short stories and thrillers. *The Accidental Plus One: Travel Tales from a Trailing Spouse* is her ninth published book.

- facebook.com/alisonripleycubittwriter
- x.com/lambertnagle
- instagram.com/alisonripleycubitt

Also by Alison Ripley Cubitt

Castles in the Air
https://mybook.to/CastlesintheAir
Misadventures in the Screen Trade
https://mybook.to/StephenConnor1
Finding a Home in Aotearoa New Zealand
https://mybook.to/FindaHomeNZ
Revolution Earth by Lambert Nagle
https://mybook.to/StephenConnor1
Nighthawks by Lambert Nagle
https://mybook.to/StephenConnor2

If you love reading and writing memoirs, join us in the We Love Memoirs Facebook group.

www.facebook.com/groups/welovememoirs

www.ingramcontent.com/pod-product-compliance
Lightning Source LLC
Chambersburg PA
CBHW030434010526
44118CB00011B/626